Guatemala
A Country Guide

Tom Barry

The Inter-Hemispheric Education Resource Center

Albuquerque, New Mexico

Guatemala

A Country Guide

Acknowledgments

Guatemala: A Country Guide is to a great extent a collective product of the Resource Center staff. Diligent research assistance came from Jenny Beatty, Joan MacLean, Felipe Montoya, Debra Preusch, and Thomas Weiss. In addition, Jenny Beatty guided the book from the manuscript page to the typeset book with her wordprocessing and formatting skills, while Debra Preusch, in addition to interviewing and research assistance, organized and oversaw the various stages of the making of this book—from making travel arrangments to dealing with the printer. Chuck Hosking and Beth Sims edited the manuscript, and Jenny Beatty proofread the book.

I would also like to thank friends and associates in Guatemala for their assistance, hospitality, and comments on the manuscript. My appreciation is also extended to several Guatemala experts in the United States who provided valuable comments on the manuscript. A book of this nature would not be possible without the ongoing information-gathering and research work of many other reporters, activists, and scholars.

Table of Contents

Introduction	**1**
Politics	**7**
Government	7
Fragile Democracy	11
Social and Economic Policies	11
Political Parties and Elections	14
The Democratization Process	15
The Left and Center-Left	16
The Center-Right	17
The Right	21
Foreign Policy	26
Dubious Neutrality	27
The Question of Belize	29
The Peace Process	29
Negotiations with the URNG	30
Human Rights	31
Military	**37**
Security Forces	37
Structure of the Armed Forces	39
The Privatization of the Military	40
The Soft Sell	41
Saving the Nation	43
Splits within the Military	44
Civil Patrols	47

The Army and the Displaced 49
Police Divisions 50
Paramilitary Groups 51
Guerrilla Opposition 52
Who They Are and What They Want 53
The Military Front 54
Talking About Peace 56

Economy 59
The State of the Economy 59
Economic Picture Darkens 61
Modern Oligarchs 62
Inside the Oligarchy 63
Agriculture 67
Land Reform 67
Traditional Exports 69
Nontraditional Exports 71
Food Production 72
Industry and Tourism 73

Society and Environment 75
Popular Organizing 75
The Clamor for Land 76
The Popular Alliance 76
Labor and Unions 79
Solidarismo: Labor/Owner Cooperation 83
Schools and Students 85
Student Movement Revives 85
The Private Alternative to USAC 87
Communications Media 87
The Daily News 89
The Electronic Media 91
The State of Health 93
Religion 95
The Catholic Church: Power, Tradition, and Change 96
The Rise of the Evangelicals 101

Nongovernmental Organizations 105
The Role of AID 106
AID in the Eighties 106
NGOs and Counterinsurgency 108
Women and Feminism 109
Native People 111
Indians and the Popular Movement 113
The Fourth World 114
Revolutionary Movement: The Indigenous Question 115
Refugees and the Internally Displaced 116
Guatemalans in the United States 117
Repatriation and Resettlement 117
Nature and Environmentalism 119
The Ravages of War 122
The Plague of Pesticides 123
The Urban Nightmare 123
Environmental Activism 124

Foreign Influence **125**
U.S Foreign Policy 125
Relations Sour and Sweeten 125
U.S. Assistance Strategy 126
Prospects for the 1990s 128
U.S. Trade and Investment 129
U.S. Economic Aid 130
Aid for Counterinsurgency 131
Nontraditional Exports, But Little to Eat 132
Private-Sector Support 133
Democracy Strengthening 133
U.S. Military Aid 136
Other Military Related Aid 138
Other Foreign Interests 140
Israel 143

Reference Notes   **145**

Appendices
    Statistics   153
    Chronology   157
    Bibliography   165
    For More Information   167

The Resource Center

The Inter-Hemispheric Education Resource Center is a private non-profit research and policy institute located in Albuquerque, New Mexico. Founded in 1979, the Resource Center produces books, policy reports, and other research about U.S. foreign relations with third world countries. Among its most popular materials are *The Central America Fact Book* and the quarterly *Bulletin* mailed to subscribers for $5 annually ($7.50 outside the United States). For a catalogue of publications, please write to the Resource Center, Box 4506, Albuquerque, NM 87196.

Board of Directors

Toney Anaya, *Former Governor of New Mexico;* Tom Barry, *Resource Center;* Blase Bonpane, *Office Of the Americas;* Fred Bronkema, *Human Rights Office, National Council of the Churches of Christ;* Ann Mari Buitrago, *Institute for Public Access to Government Information;* Noam Chomsky, *Massachusetts Institute of Technology;* Dr. Charles Clements, *SatelLife;* Rev. Joe Eldridge, *Methodist Missionary;* Dr. Wallace Ford, *New Mexico Conference of Churches;* Robert Foxworth, *Actor and Director;* Antonio González, *Southwest Voter Research Institute;* Don Hancock, *Southwest Research and Information Center;* Joy Harjo, *Poet and Screenwriter;* Joyce Hill, *United Methodist Church;* Ruth Hubbard, *Biologist and Writer;* Patricia Hynds, *Maryknoll Lay Missioner;* Mary MacArthur, *Cultural Worker;* Jennifer Manríquez, *Community Activist;* John Nichols, *Author;* Debra Preusch, *Resource Center;* Thomas E. Quigley, *U.S. Catholic Conference;* Margaret Randall, *Writer and Photographer;* James Ridgeway, *Village Voice;* Frank I. Sánchez, *Partnership for Democracy;* Beth Wood, *Central America Information Center.* (Organizations listed for identification purposes only.)

Guatemala

MEXICO

El Petén

BELIZE

Caribbean Sea

Huehuetenango

Alta Verapaz

Quiché

Izabal

San Marcos

Baja Verapaz

Zacapa

HONDURAS

Totoni-capán

Quezalte-nango

Sololá

El Progreso

Chimalte-nango

Guate-mala

Jalapa

Chiquimula

Retalhuleu

Such

Sacate-péquez

Escuintla

Jutiapa

Santa Rosa

EL SALVADOR

Pacific Ocean

Inforpress Centroamericana

Introduction

Scores of anxious Indian men and women were bussed into Guatemala City from their highland villages. Many had never before been to Guatemala City. The occasion was the Day of La Raza, established by the government to honor the Indian heritage and culture of Guatemala, a country in which over half the population is Indian. Gathered in this alien urban setting, the Indian contingents—dressed in their finest and most traditional clothing—were on display. Each of the village *cofradías* (organizations of community elders) performed traditional dances and skits as they paraded slowly through the downtown streets in route to the Central Plaza. Many of the paraders were barefooted, their deeply calloused feet seemingly unaffected by heat rising from the city streets.

The plaza soon filled with the colors and artistry of the *huipiles* (blouses) and *cortes* (wrap-around skirts) of the Indian women. The men were dressed mostly in white and were wearing their best straw hats for the event. At nightfall, an elaborate fireworks spectacle filled the plaza with a dazzling kaleidoscope of sound and light. Then, as the president stepped out onto the balcony of the National Palace, all the Indian men removed their straw hats to pay proper homage to *El Señor Presidente*.

In January 1986 the presidency was turned over to a politician elected in a national election. The president may now be a civilian, but little else about Guatemala seems to be changing. The society is still sharply divided between Indians and *ladinos* (*mestizo* non-Indians). What was unhealthy in society before January 1986 seems only to have worsened. What was beautiful is being lost at a more rapid pace. Barefoot peasants, killings in the night, and an economy steeped in feudalism were all part of the Guatemala described by Miguel Angel Asturias in his classic novel, *El Señor Presidente*. The tragedy and terror that trapped Guatemalan society in that 1933 novel about military and oligarchic rule continue to burden life in the "New Guatemala."

* * *

Guatemala, the most populated country of Central America, stuns visitors with its natural and human beauty. From black-sand beaches and fertile plains along the Pacific coast, the land sweeps up into the rugged highland region. Marking this dramatic division between the coastal lowlands and the western highlands is a wall of 23 majestic volcanoes, many of them still fuming, that stretch along the central highlands. Like most of Central America, Guatemala is located in a zone of extreme geological instability. Guatemala City and the old capital city of Antigua have been severely damaged by earthquakes at least 15 times since the 16th century.[1]

On a clear day one can witness both topographical worlds from the peak of the extinct Volcán de Agua. Looking toward the Pacific Ocean, the country's economic heartland fans out before you. In the distance, vast agroexport plantations extend to the sea. Closer in, as the terrain rises, the folds of the hills and the volcano itself are covered with the deep green of coffee bushes. Antigua, which lies in the shadow of Agua, is the colonial capital and produces some of the world's finest coffee. Looking east toward Guatemala City, there appear occasional flashes of fire and brimstone from the fitful Pacaya volcano.

Turning away from the sea are the highlands or *altiplano*. Throughout these mountains live the indigenous peoples of Guatemala. For centuries, they have survived tending their corn and beans on small mountain plots. Market days announce themselves with an explosion of color and community as Indian families trickle out of the mountains to buy and sell in the plaza of the local municipality.

Poverty and hunger stalk these mountains. From the youngest to the oldest, the focus of daily life is survival. Young girls walk for miles carrying heavy jars of water. By the side of the road, old men, like pack animals, carry impossibly heavy burdens of firewood and agricultural produce.

The *altiplano* is stained with the blood of massacres from a counter-insurgency campaign that swept through the mountains in the early 1980s. It is a region whose sad story is told by the proliferation of army outposts and the scorched remains of Indian villages. For the most part, the voices of its Indian inhabitants have been silenced by terror and trauma.

Beyond the highlands lies the Northern Transverse Strip (FTN), a band of jungle that spans the top of the departments of Alta Verapaz, Quiché, and Huehuetenango. Settled only during the last twenty years, the FTN has become known as the Zone of Generals, owing to the wholesale land-grabbing by military officers. Like the *altiplano*, it is one of the country's main conflictive zones. The army is trying to assert control over the FTN with road-building projects and counterinsurgency sweeps, but elusive guerrillas have largely managed to stop the advance of the roads and disappear into the jungle in the face of army offensives and bombing raids.

Jutting out like some unnatural appendage is the department of Petén, a vast expanse of tropical forest that was once a center for the Mayan civilization. From the heights of the Tikal pyramids, the Petén seems a never-ending carpet of tropical green. But flying over the region, it is not the tropical forests that draw your attention but the spreading deforestation by timber companies, cattle ranchers, and slash-and-burn peasant farmers. It is here in the Petén where the Kaibiles, an elite counterinsurgency battalion, have their base.

In the northeast, Guatemala touches the Caribbean in the steamy department of Izabal, the center of the Del Monte banana enclave. Stretching south along the eastern border is what is known in Guatemala as the *oriente*, an arid, often desolate region populated by a *ladino* (non-Indian) peasant class. The torrid departments of Zacapa, Chiquimula, Progreso, Jalapa, Santa Rosa, and Jutiapa provide the country with its police and military officers. The *oriente* has also been the traditional base of the National Liberation Movement (MLN), Guatemala's extreme rightwing party.

* * *

Modern history in Guatemala dates back to 1944, the year when longtime dictator General Jorge Ubico retired and a successor regime was overthrown by a reformist alliance of military officers, students, professionals, businessmen, and politicians.[2] For ten years Guatemala experimented with democracy, social reforms, and economic modernization.tiontion A violent coup in 1954—supported by the CIA, rightwing politicians, the Catholic hierarchy, and the oligarchy—brought that period to an abrupt end. For the last 35 years the country has suffered the legacy of that abortion of democracy and reform.

The coup carried out by Colonel Carlos Castillo Armas and his CIA backers reinstalled oligarchic and military control in Guatemala, melded now with the ideology of anticommunism and national security. Many hoped that the 1985 elections that brought Vinicio Cerezo into the National Palace would return the light of reason and progress to a country darkened by decades of rightwing extremism, military rule, and oligarchic conservatism. It was the hope of many that a civilian Christian Democratic government would return Guatemala to the path optimistically initiated in 1944 by Juan José Arévalo and the October Revolution.[3]

But the past three and a half decades are not so easily erased. There is much to overcome. In the days of Jorge Ubico, the military was a small, unprofessional gendarmerie that served largely at the pleasure of the landed elite. Today, the military is a highly professional and independent force whose tentacles extend to the smallest mountain village. More than a fighting force, it directs political and economic affairs and has developed its own sophisticated theories of national security and development.

The principal protagonists of the 1954 coup—the right wing and the country's reactionary agroexport oligarchy on the domestic front and the United States on the international front—still loom as major obstacles to real change in Guatemala. The oligarchy and the extreme rightwing political parties in league with factions of the army are ever vigilant against creeping socialism, threatening and even occasionally attempting coups to keep the country in line with their authoritarian beliefs. The U.S. government, while no longer such a principled opponent of agrarian reform, would consider any popular movement for major structural changes as a threat to its own security. Since 1983 Washington has, for the most part, danced in tune with the army's project for political stabilization. U.S. aid has focused its economic aid on bolstering the private-sector elite and export economy, while paying only lip service to the need for "broad-based" and "equitable" development.

Tourists are told that Guatemala is the land of "eternal spring." Characteristic of the black humor of the country, students joke that it is the land of eternal repression. Indeed, repression seems an almost natural part of the climate in Guatemala. So final is the repression that the country has no political prisoners—there are just bodies and disappearances. So pervasive is this repression that the army has infiltrated the communities themselves with so-called "voluntary civil-defense patrols."

Fear, suspicion, and paranoia are almost endemic to Guatemalans. Politics is a subject of conversation for only the most trusted of friends. Phones are assumed to be "intervened" by the security forces. Personal information—where one works or lives—is closely guarded in Guatemala. Despite the institution of civilian government, many Guatemalans still go about life always looking over their shoulder to see if they are being followed or watched. Underlying the current political opening is a widespread concern that it is drawing inevitably to a close and that the pall of unrelenting repression is once again falling over Guatemala. As the decade drew to a close, Catholic Archbishop Próspero Penados del Barrio warned that Guatemala was being overtaken by "a climate of anxiety, a feeling of capsizing."[4]

Guatemala is a country rife with contrasts. In Antigua, an international tourist class escapes the industrialized world in a fantasyland of colonial churches, cobblestoned streets, an indigenous culture, pastry shops, and vegetarian pizza. The stone walls of the city, however, hide a brutal economy where Indian laborers work for a dollar or two a day picking coffee for oligarchs. Tourists rush to Guatemala to dip into the past and to savor the beauty of the native artisans, blind to the economic cruelty that pervades the society.

Deep in the country's interior, army psychological-operations teams show videos about the threat of communist "delinquents" and "terrorists" to Indians who, having never seen television before, are more mesmerized by the medium than the message. Civil Affairs promoters from the army initiate patriotic educational campaigns and organize beauty contests of teenage Indian girls dressed in their traditional *traje* to inaugurate "model villages" in an attempt to integrate Indian communities into the "national life." In the cities, Indian men cut mansion lawns with their machetes, while pentecostal preachers trudge through the city dumps, salvaging the souls of those who fight for scraps of garbage alongside legions of vultures.

Guatemala is an armed camp, from the countryside where the local military garrisons preside over political and social life to the cities where armed power is shared by the security forces and the criminal bands. The oligarchs and military-linked death squads are the other forces that maintain their power and concept of law and order with weapons and terror. While it is the poor who are the main victims of this culture of violence, even the elite live in an environment of fear as the result of frequent political feuds, threats of extortion, and factional rivalries.

Life, which has always been lived on the edge in Guatemala, is becoming increasingly precarious. For most Guatemalans, rising human rights violations and increased repression are of lesser concern than the constant death and suffering inflicted by the society's grossly uneven economic structures. More Guatemalans die of preventable diseases than as a result of political violence. According to a statistical study by the University of San Carlos, 86 percent of Guatemalans live in poverty, up from 63 percent in 1981.[5] During the 1980s the standard of living declined 20 percent.[6] Each year 42,000 children die of preventable or curable diseases.[7] While Guatemala has shifted politically, it remains entrenched in its benighted systems of land tenure and labor exploitation. The misery resulting from repression and structural injustices is compounded by a high population growth rate.

A small guerrilla movement presents a persistent challenge to this society of generals and oligarchs. The leftist guerrilla coalition calls for revolutionary changes in the nation's economic structures and a broadening of democracy. Failure of the government and army to modernize the economy and politically stabilize the country could result in a widening civil war. Given the starkly divided nature of Guatemalan society and the uncompromising power of the army and private elite, such a civil war would likely be characterized by sharp race and class alliances. And, as one Guatemalan journalist observed, "War in Guatemala will be fought in color, not black and white like in El Salvador. Perhaps a million will die."

For the moment, however, Guatemala is maintaining a tenuous political and economic stability. Civilian rule returned to Guatemala in the mid-1980s following a brutal, almost genocidal counterinsurgency campaign which nearly smashed the guerrilla movement during the first part of the decade. It is a top-down style of formal democracy whose main proponents are the military high command and the political elite. U.S. government-financed forums to discuss the democratization process are held in luxury hotels, while the military seeks international aid for its own political studies institute. This process of democratization has proved shallow. Proponents pointed out that labor confederations, peasants demanding land, and human rights advocates were permitted to demonstrate in front of the National Palace for the first time in many years. But the democracy instituted in 1985 has not meant that *El Señor Presidente* is necessarily listening to those demands, or that human rights violations have significantly decreased. Nor has the reputed democratization meant that two main forces in Guatemala — the army and the oligarchy — have ceded their power to the people.

Chapter 1

Politics

Government

The National Palace, the center of government in Guatemala, has for most of its long history been largely an adjunct of the military high command. From 1954 to 1986 only one civilian president (Julio César Méndez Montenegro) occupied the palace. Yet even his regime (1966-1970) was guided by the dictates of the military.

Although military rule is a tradition in Guatemala, so are elections.[1] Every four years, the military would select its candidate, hold an election, and declare its candidate the winner. By the early 1980s this system began breaking down as elements within the military began to question the validity and wisdom of government by direct military rule. In 1982 a group of dissident officers, led by General Efraín Ríos Montt (retired) seized the National Palace and ousted the handpicked successor of former president General Fernando Romeo Lucas García.

A month after the coup, the military government took a decidedly new approach to the counterinsurgency war. While continuing the scorched-earth tactics of the predecessor regime, the Ríos Montt government began to incorporate a developmentalist and nation-building side to the military effort. This new vision was outlined in the National Security and Development Plan (PNSD), decreed as law in April 1982. According to this plan, "The war is to be combated on all fronts: on the military and the political, but above all on the socioeconomic. The minds of the population are the principal objective." The PNSD addressed four problem areas undermining national stability:

1. Political Stability: The need to legitimize the government on both local and international levels. To do this, the military recognized that it needed to take steps to return government to a legal framework, meaning a new constitution, elections, and the revival of political parties.

2. Economic Stability: The need to pull the country out of economic recession and to address the severe poverty of the rural population.
3. Psycho-Social Stability: The need to contain the advances of the guerrillas among peasants, Indians, and the illiterate.
4. Military Stability: The need to defeat the armed subversion.[2]

The PNSD set the guidelines for the evolution of government in the 1980s. It established politics as an extension of war, and government as

---

From Victory in the Mountains

Victory 82: The army continued the scorched-earth campaign of terror and massacres initiated during the Lucas García regime in 1981, while forming Civil Defense Patrols (PAC) to tighten its grip on the rural population.

Firmness 83: The development component of counterinsurgency swung into action this year with the creation of development poles, model villages, and inter-institutional coordinators. According to the army, this campaign set about "integrating public service institutions in the struggle against terrorism to vitalize the work and accelerate the task of pacification of the country."

Institutional Re-encounter 84: The army expanded the concept of "security and development" to include political stabilization. Recognizing the need for a legal framework for the counterinsurgency war, the army sponsored elections for a Constituent Assembly whose function was to formulate a new constitution. Additionally, the military assigned itself the task of leading the reconstruction of the country and started to address the problem of the displaced population.

National Stability 85: The army described this year's goals as follows: "During the development of the [1985] campaign plan, military operations were intensified. Governmental institutions directed their activities toward the support of the socioeconomic programs and paid close attention to the political developments, motivating the active forces in the country to achieve massive participation in the upcoming elections." This "return to constitutionality" was designed "to consolidate the democratic system of life, to develop the nation's economy, strengthen government institutions, create a feeling of security in the population, and attempt to gain international recognition and support for the nation and its government."

an instrument of a national-stability project defined by the military. The plan for security and development moved Guatemala away from a military-controlled "national-security state" to a national-security civilian government, also controlled by the military.[3] The course of this evolution of war and politics can be seen in the military's annual designations of objectives and priorities, shifting priority from the war effort and increasing focus on politics and the stabilization of government.[4] (See Box)

to Consolidation of Government

National Consolidation 86: The election of a civilian president and increasing international respect and assistance marked the success of the army's democratization strategy. Now the army moved to consolidate the Guatemalan state. Defense Minister General Hector Alejandro Gramajo observed: "In Guatemala, politics ought to be the extension of war. We are still ready for battle, only we are fighting on a broader horizon within a democratic framework, and we are renovating fighting methods."

The army has continued to pin a new name to each year: "Campaign Plan 87" was followed by "Determination 88." New military and political strategies have been adopted, always guided by the principle that "politics ought to be the extension of war." New efforts have been launched to assert military control over the entire displaced population and to defeat the Guatemalan National Revolutionary Unity (URNG) forces, both militarily and strategically. The army spearheaded the creation of multi-sectoral teams to spur development projects in conflictive zones.

Recognizing the need to incorporate all sectors (private, political, popular, etc.) into its strategies, the army created a new political institute called the Center for Strategic Studies for National Stability (ESTNA), sponsored public forums to discuss democratization, and otherwise tried to popularize the notion that its vision of national stability is in the best interests of the entire society. At a September 1989 roundtable sponsored by ESTNA, Defense Minister Gramajo said that stability is threatened by those military and business figures who hold to the "iron hand" national-security policy in vogue prior to 1982. Today, he said, the emphasis is on national stability which seeks harmony between various power blocs. With the obligatory retirement of Gramajo in May 1990 and his replacement by General Bolaños, this model of "state stability" was likely to remain the dominant.

The Ríos Montt coup injected a new dynamism into the military's response to the guerrilla threat and popular rebellion in the highlands. As president, Ríos Montt also took measures to inject a new legitimacy in government through the creation of a Council of State, with representatives from various social sectors. Ríos Montt, however, was not the ideal coordinator for the military's stabilization efforts. His evangelical religious convictions alienated many important elements of Guatemalan society and did little to break down the country's international isolation.

A year and a half after the coup that installed Ríos Montt as president, the National Palace was the scene of another military coup, this time replacing Ríos Montt in August 1983 with his Minister of Defense General Oscar Humberto Mejía Víctores. The Mejía Víctores coup put the traditional military hierarchy back into command and immediately began the process to institute formal civilian rule — one of the principles of the security and development plan. Elections for the Constituent Assembly were held in 1984, and a new constitution was approved. In late 1985 the military sponsored fraud-free elections for the presidency and seats in the new National Congress.

Vinicio Cerezo received the blue presidential sash from General Mejía Víctores in January 1986, and began his five-year presidential term backed by the military high command and by a clear majority of Christian Democrats in the newly constituted unicameral National Congress. The 100-member National Congress is composed of 75 representatives who are directly elected and 25 who receive their seats based on proportional representation among the political parties. In mid-1990, the National Election Board (TSE) approved a congressional recommendation that the National Congress be expanded to 125 members to reflect population growth. The country is divided into 22 departments administered by governors appointed by the president.[5] The departments include 326 municipal governments (*municipios*) whose mayors and town councils are popularly elected.[6]

Thus, as originally set forth in the PNSD, civilian rule was reinstituted in Guatemala. A formal democracy was established whose limits were clear from the beginning: there would be no room for the revolutionary left and the army would be its guardian and final arbiter. The military also remained in direct administrative control over all conflictive areas in the country.

Fragile Democracy

International reports commonly describe Guatemala as a "fragile democracy." The term accurately conveys that civilian government does indeed hang in the balance – its stability threatened by potential military coups, guerrilla insurgency, economic crisis, oligarchic reaction, and its own failure to build popular support. Nonetheless, to describe the country as a "fragile democracy" hides more than it reveals about the nature of government in Guatemala.

Democratic government was not established by popular demand but by military dictate. Elections, constitutional rule, and a civilian chief-of-state were not hard-won freedoms but gifts of the military – which may be taken back at any time. The constant threat of a military coup is often regarded as the main threat to civilian rule. The fragility of the civilian government has more to do with the position of the military as the self-appointed creator, adviser, and protector of the democratization process. It is this dependency on the military that limits the impact of civilian government and will ultimately undermine its very existence. As President Cerezo, himself, observed: "If anyone is responsible for this democratizing process and willing to consolidate it, it is the army."[7]

The critical role of the military in setting the democratization process in motion has never been in doubt. There was, however, widespread hope that the Cerezo government would take measures to build popular support for government and would seek more independence from the military. But this was not the case. Instead, the bases of support for the civilian government steadily contracted so that it became increasingly dependent on the continued goodwill of the military high command.

Social and Economic Policies

The initial overture of the Cerezo government toward the achievement of popular support was its policy of consensus (*concertación*). But this attempt to build wide-ranging support for the government's economic and social policies proved a failure. Based on the economics of austerity and price liberalization, the *concertación* initiative was aimed almost exclusively at the private-sector elite represented by the Coordinating Committee of Agricultural, Commercial, Industrial, and Financial Associations (CACIF), the traditional oligarchic voice. Excluded from decisions about economic policy were the social sectors that were to suffer most from these purported stabilization policies.[8]

Yet even this narrow effort to gain the confidence and support of the private sector ultimately failed as CACIF and other business organizations soon became disaffected with the government. While demanding inclusion in the process of economic policymaking, CACIF is not in the habit of compromising. The leading voices of the private sector have objected to all government attempts to broaden the country's tax base, to stabilize prices of basic goods, and to increase the government's budget for social services.

For the most part, the Cerezo government instituted economic policies designed to please the private sector and international lending agencies. But, like the army, it recognized that the basic needs of the poor also needed to be addressed to maintain national stability. This is what both the Cerezo government and the army called the country's "social debt." In addressing this social debt, the Cerezo government did not propose structural reforms that would target the causes for the extreme polarization of Guatemalan society. Rather, it called for an extension of social-service programs (education, housing, health care) and economic development projects that stressed micro-enterprise formation. Not up for discussion were more profound measures — agrarian reform, a just tax structure that decreases indirect taxes (which weigh disproportionately on the poor), or substantial increases in minimum wage levels.

For the private sector, any discussion of social debt rings of socialism and class confrontation, and it will hear none of it. In the face of government and army proposals for expanded public-sector programs, the private sector countered that such plans would generate more corruption and flounder due to the notorious inefficiency of government agencies. The business elite also contended that the Cerezo government's plans for development councils and the like would be abused as patronage vehicles for the Christian Democratic Party.

Among the popular sectors, there is support for increased government attention to the needs of the poor majority, but the Christian Democratic approach was criticized as being paternalistic, superficial, and characterized by broken promises. In particular, the government's failure to respect a pact made with the popular movement in April 1988 for wage increases and a price freeze greatly disillusioned representatives of the popular movement.

Another persistent concern has been that the civilian government's response to socioeconomic problems is merely an extension of the army's own developmentalism and related "psycho-social" operations. Like the military, the government agreed that the priority for government development and social-services programs should be the conflictive zones. The Cerezo government supported the military's own program of development poles, model villages, inter-institutional coordinators, and civil defense patrols — under the facelifted guises of development centers, development villages, development councils, and voluntary self-defense committees.

Though instigated by the military, there is little doubt that elections and a civilian government represent a measurable step forward in the country's political evolution. But in its five-year term the Cerezo government failed to use this political opening to link itself more closely with the popular sectors and to take measures to improve socioeconomic conditions. Even talk of addressing the "social debt" was dropped by 1989. As a result, at the end of Cerezo's term there was little popular support for the civilian government. Electoral democracy had been instituted but it showed itself to be corrupt and in league with the military and business elite.

The country's political stability hangs in the balance. The 1990 elections offered little source of hope, with the contending parties offering slogans about "law," "order," and "honesty" but differing little from one another in terms of their conservative economic principles and allegiance to the military-controlled state. So disgusted were many people, particularly among the urban middle class but also among the rural population, that there was surprising support for military candidates, including General Ríos Montt. These electoral politics were played out against a frightening background of increasing human rights violations, a downsliding economy, a visible increase in poverty, and a resurgent guerrilla war.

By mid-1990 the Guatemalan government was itself a victim of the economic crisis and the four-year sacking of government ministries by the Christian Democrats. At one point mail service to Europe and other foreign destinations was suspended because the government did not have the funds to pay the shipping charges. Failing to pay its dues, the government could no longer vote in the United Nations. Guatemalan embassies and consulates around the world were closed.

At the end of the Cerezo administration, the government was hard put to point to anything that it could call its legacy. Local and regional development plans had fallen flat, health ministries officials were found to have put U.S. economic aid into their own pockets, and social services were cut to the bone. Unlike preceding regimes, the Cerezo government did not even have any large infrastructure projects to call its own. The Christian Democratic Party could say that it kept government in civilian hands for five years, but the continued existence of a civilian government was more due to the commitment of the military high command than to the resolve of the Christian Democrats.

During its five years the Cerezo administration committed itself to the state stability model of government, trying to balance the need for social stability with the demands of the private sector. With only six months left in office, Cerezo found himself with a government that had largely adopted the neoliberal option but was nonetheless heavily criticized by the private sector. With no strong reformist parties to its left and in the absence of both a strong popular movement and revolutionary option, the government seemed certain to move yet further to the right and deeper into grasp of neoliberal reformers.

Political Parties and Elections

A casual visitor might conclude from the roadside display of political artifacts that Guatemala must be a vibrant democracy. Whenever one turns a bend in the road, the colors, abbreviations, and flags of one or more political parties are painted on the exposed rocks and cliffs. Bridges, bus stops, and even the highways themselves bear these emblems. In Guatemala, political parties are not accustomed to paying for billboard space, instead simply taking advantage of any exposed surface as an outlet for their political fervor.

Electioneering is not a new fad in Guatemala. Political campaigning also occurred during the long succession of military regimes that date back to 1954. It has represented part of the jockeying for power by different sectors of the military and oligarchy. The National Liberation Movement (MLN), the self-denominated "party of organized violence," has a long tradition of political campaigning and of proliferating its red-white-and-blue colors. In some areas of the country, there is scarcely a bus stand or large roadside rock without a painted MLN flag. Even its Guatemala City headquarters, which some call the "castle of death," is painted in flag colors.

Political parties also have a tradition of taking their campaigns to the people. They do this in car caravans filled with party faithful waving party flags and scattering party propaganda leaflets all about the villages through which they pass. To dramatize and facilitate its car caravaning, the MLN attaches pine branches to the vehicles' front bumpers to sweep away the nails and other puncturing devices that might have been strewn across the road to hinder the advance of the party. Another tradition is the political violence that precedes and accompanies electoral campaigns. Kidnappings, death threats, and beatings are as much a part of campaigning in Guatemala as bullhorns and posters.

The Democratization Process

Along with the tradition of elections and political parties in Guatemala, there is also a tradition of electoral fraud, military control, and a decided lack of pluralism. This latter tradition has proved costly to the country's international image and its ability to attract foreign aid. In 1983, the military high command embarked the country on a tentative process of democratization, having decided that the political and economic stability of Guatemala would be better served by a civilian government chosen in pluralistic elections. In 1984 elections were held for the Constituent Assembly and a year later Guatemalans went to the polls to elect their next president. Winning 68 percent of the vote, Vinicio Cerezo Arévalo took office in January 1986 for a five-year term.

Compared with previous presidential elections, the 1985 balloting was free of fraud and relatively open. For many Guatemalans, the election was viewed as a chance to set Guatemala on a new path that would free the country from the terror of the past. Others, however, were less hopeful, pointing out that the last civilian president, Julio César Méndez Montenegro (1966-1970), was completely controlled by the military.

The installation of a civilian government did enhance significantly the country's reputation in international circles and opened important political maneuvering room within the country as well. But many basic characteristics of the political world in Guatemala did not change. The guerrilla opposition continued to be excluded from the political process, and the military continued to be the final arbiter of political and economic change. As in the past, political parties remained largely divorced from the popular movement, each depending on its own narrow base of financial and citizen support.

The country's political spectrum ranges from the ultra-right to the armed left. Both political poles defend the need for political violence: the right, to defend the country's institutions; the left, to change them. While the ultra-right participates in the political process, the armed left has been excluded and repressed, with most of the legal political parties being clustered on the right.

The first round of the 1990 presidential elections were scheduled for November with a probable second round planned for January 1991 for the two leading candidates if no one presidential contender received 50 percent plus one vote in the first round. The next president is scheduled to take office in late January 1991.

The ruling Guatemalan Christian Democratic Party (DCG) approached the elections badly divided and with its popular support steadily sinking. Nonetheless it was the party with the most extensive infrastructure, especially in rural areas, and could count on a substantial patronage vote. The center-right National Union Center Party (UCN), which lost to the DCG in the second round of the 1985 elections, hoped that its persistent criticism of the Cerezo government and its ample publicity would catapult it to the presidency in 1991. The extreme right wing and the oligarchy were in disarray at the beginning of the campaigning but hoped to duplicate the victories of other rightwing parties throughout Central America. Casting a particularly ominous shadow over the campaign were the candidacies of two retired generals.

As the elections neared there was little popular interest or enthusiasm visible, even though the electoral process would open the way for the first transition between civilian governments in forty years. Instead, deepening human rights abuses, deteriorating socioeconomic conditions, and a widening counterinsurgency war were the issues that dominated public concern.

The Left and Center-Left

The **Guatemalan Workers Party (PGT)**, the country's official communist party, has functioned clandestinely since 1954. Two tendencies of the party—PGT Central Committee and PGT Nucleus—have at various times been associated with the URNG guerrilla coalition. The PGT Nucleus was a founding member of the URNG in 1982 but eventually left. The URNG was later joined by the PGT Central Committee. In early 1989, a reformist offshoot of the party, PGT-6th of January, demanded the incorporation of *glasnost* into the Guatemalan communist party. It is seeking to join a coalition with another leftist group called the Revolutionary October Party (OR). The OR, composed primarily of former members of the Guatemalan Army of the Poor (EGP) guerrillas, believes that the URNG focus on military methods is insufficient. It places strong emphasis on women's, ethnic, and environmental issues.[9]

The **Democratic Socialist Party (PSD)**, which disbanded following the assassination of its founder Alberto Fuentes Mohr and 15 other party activists during the Lucas García regime, re-established itself in 1985 to take advantage of the political opening afforded by the democratization process.[10] Associated internationally with the Socialist International, the PSD is more a social-democratic party than a socialist one. It stands to the right of the National Revolutionary Movement (MNR) in El Salvador and to the left of the National Liberation Party (PLN) in Costa Rica, both of which are also members of the Socialist International.

The PSD's leader is Mario Solórzano, who represents the more conservative or centrist faction of the party. Solórzano articulates a reformist rather than a socialist political philosophy. According to Solórzano, the PSD promotes the "full development of capitalism, a modern not exploitative capitalism, to replace the feudalism that currently imprisons Guatemala." The PSD was the original proponent of a "Social Pact" between government, private sector, political parties, and labor. In 1988, this reformist vision split the party as its secretary general, Luis Zurita, left the PSD, charging that Solórzano was catering to elites rather than organizing the masses and that the party should be socialist, not social democratic.[11]

Typical of the opportunism that characterizes centrist politics in Guatemala, the PSD proclaimed René de León Schlotter as its presidential candidate. Representing a dissident faction of the DCG called the Popular Alliance (AP-5), de León was regarded by the PSD as their best chance to win enough votes in the national elections to guarantee the party's national registry and its representation in Congress. De León, although long a leader of the DCG's conservative wing, adopted a left-leaning discourse to criticize the government after having failed to win the DCG's nomination.

As the election campaign opened it was clear that the political parties of the left were weak, without popular support, and largely unprincipled. By opportunistically joining alliances with parties and political figures of the center-right, the organized political left lost what was left of their credibility among the popular movement. This void on the left side of the political arena will make it all the more difficult for the URNG to enter the electoral process.

The Center-Right

The **Guatemalan Christian Democratic Party (DCG)** is the only political party that can be considered centrist. The DCG was founded as a rightist party in 1955, in the shadow of the 1954 coup. For the last twenty years, however, the party has assumed a reformist image, posing as the centrist alternative between revolutionary change and extreme rightwing reaction. It has been consistent in its call for the modernization of capitalism as "a better way to fight communism."

The DCG is a product of the Christian Democratic movement in Europe, which emerged as an alternative to the more communist and social-democratic parties that sought power in post-World War II Europe. This movement was based on the social teachings of the Catholic church, expounded for the first time in the late 19th century by Pope Leo

XIII in his *Rerum Novarum* encyclical. This Christian social philosophy taught that economic classes could work in harmony. To achieve this goal, socialism, with its philosophy of inevitable class conflict, had to be opposed, while capitalism should be reformed to insure social justice.[12]

Despite its support for social reforms, the DCG has remained a strictly electoral party, eschewing coalitions with the popular movement. Although it has lost dozens of party activists to political repression, the DCG has been steadfast in its commitment to the electoral path. In fact, the pursuit of political power increasingly distanced the party from the popular movement, shifting it ever closer to the very elements of society responsible for the country's main social ills.

In its first three years of power, the DCG demonstrated both its inability and unwillingness to seek social reforms on behalf of the poor majority. The party was swept into power in a wave of popular enthusiasm for the prospects of civilian rule and peaceful change, rather than on the basis provided by its own national infrastructure. Instead of trying to shape this mandate into a strong base of popular support, the Cerezo government sought to establish stronger links with the military and private sector, even to the extent of alienating those who had voted the party into office. When the party occasionally did attempt to meet popular demands, it inevitably withdrew those offers in the face of sanctions and warnings by the military and the private sector.

In its years as the ruling party the DCG, directed by Cerezo, was characterized by its political astuteness, its adept international public relations, and its opportunism. Benefiting from a generous supply of international aid and goodwill, the Cerezo government managed to keep the other political parties off-balance and divided. Although the country remained mired in civil war and human rights violations, Cerezo maintained warm international relations based on his promise to keep Guatemala on the "transition to democracy."

The successful ascent to power of the DCG and Vinicio Cerezo was due largely to its opportunistic alliance with the military and sectors of the right wing. From its earliest years, the DCG formed alliances with such ultra-right parties as the Anti-Communist Unification Party (PUA) and has a long tradition of backing military candidates for president. In 1974, General Efraín Ríos Montt, the presidential candidate of a reformist coalition that included the DCG and the social-democratic parties of Fuentes Mohr and Manuel Colom Argueta, was denied the presidency in a fraudulent election. Despite this experience, the DCG persisted in its quest for political power, fielding candidates again in 1978 and 1982, thereby bestowing a continued credibility to the electoral process.

Through its support of active and retired military candidates, the DCG gradually came to regard the military as a natural ally in the democratization and modernization process. This sentiment was clearly argued by DCG Secretary General Vinicio Cerezo in his 1977 essay entitled *The Army: An Alternative*:

> We must tear down the barriers that impede communication between two of the national forces that can rely on organization, discipline, and progressive ideology. They are the Army and the Christian Democratic Party....The present social, economic, and political conditions suggest that there will be no positive solution unless the two sectors UNITE and make a gigantic and combined effort to reorganize and reorient the country.[13]

Its status as ruling party greatly strengthened the DCG. As the government party, the DCG was able to build a network of supporters linked to jobs and government programs. In marked contrast to its main competitor, the UCN, the Christian Democrats, after assuming the reins of power, established a relatively strong party infrastructure in rural Guatemala. Yet its position in government also exposed the basically conservative and opportunistic nature of the party, considerably undermining initial popular enthusiasm. Government corruption and the deepening economic crisis also weigh heavily on the party's prospects for a second term.

The main party figures have been Vinicio Cerezo, René de León Schlotter, Alfonso Cabrera, and Rodolfo Paiz Andrade. A fifth figure, Danilo Barillas, was assassinated by unidentified assailants in August 1989. Cerezo, previously the leader of the party's more progressive wing, adopted a more conservative political posture after inheriting the presidential sash. Cerezo assumed control of the party from DCG patriarch René de León Schlotter, who has represented the more conservative faction and served as president of the Christian Democratic International for eight years. De León tried unsuccessfully to establish a new base of political power through the Ministry of Development and the CGT labor confederation. Cerezo's decision to promote the candidacy of Alfonso Cabrera Hidalgo, who served as Minister of Foreign Relations and as the party's secretary general, embittered de León supporters. The fourth key figure within the DCG, Paiz Andrade, a personal friend of Cerezo's and a member of the powerful Paiz Ayala family, served as a contact between the party and the private sector.

As in El Salvador, the Christian Democrats in Guatemala began to splinter before the end of their first term in office. Most of the infighting resulted from Cerezo's efforts to push forward the candidacy of Alfonso

Cabrera for the 1990 elections. Cabrera, a former school teacher, has accumulated a personal fortune through his political career. Cabrera polished the party machine, the only political infrastructure with a national reach and an organization capable of drumming up national grassroots support. But a reputation of corruption and association with narcotraffickers, including his two brothers, handicapped the Cabrera candidacy as did his uncharismatic, party-hack image. Supporters of de León complained that the nominating process was fraudulent and refused to recognize the legitimacy of the Cabrera candidacy. Cabrera supporters struck back, brutalizing the supporters and family of de León. Besides the bitter dispute between the Cabrera and de León factions, the party also suffered from the emergence or resuscitation of party offshoots, including the Popular Alliance (AP-5), whose secretary general was forced into exile by death threats, and the Movement for the Recuperation of the Christian Democrat's Ideological Identity. Government corruption, economic chaos, worsening socioeconomic conditions, and escalating political violence weigh heavily on the party's prospects for a second term.

Hoping to attract the progressive and anti-right vote, the Cabrera campaign integrated such center-left figures as Padre Andrés Girón and Luis Zurita, formerly of the PSD, into the DCG slate.

The **Revolutionary Party (PR)**, founded in 1957 after the death of Castillo Armas by former militants of the revolutionary parties of the 1944-1954 era, has been directed since its beginning by its most conservative elements (members of the Popular Liberator Front). In 1959, the party expelled its leftists. The party won national office in 1966 with Julio César Méndez Montenegro as presidential candidate. The unrelenting repression which has characterized political life in Guatemala for the last two and half decades began during the Montenegro government. In 1978 the PR allied itself with the rightwing Institutional Democratic Party (PID) to win (fraudulently) with candidate Romeo Lucas, thereby beginning the most corrupt and bloody government the country had yet known. In 1990 the PR initially hoped to gain power through the candidacy of Fernando Andrade Díaz Durán, who withdrew from the race even before it had officially begun. Also initially backing the Andrade candidacy were the center-right Democratic Party of National Cooperation (PDCN) and the National Renewal Party (PNR).

By the standards of Guatemala, the PR and Andrade are located in the center-right of the political spectrum. Both, however, have strong connections with the military and oligarchy. During the Cerezo government, Andrade represented the country at the United Nations. He was at first a DCG party member and has worked closely with the party and the Social Christian Student Front (FESC). He co-founded the Bank of the Quetzal and married into the wealthy Falla coffee family. Andrade served as a key adviser to the military regimes of Lucas García and Mejía Víctores (for whom he served as Minister of Foreign Relations) and was the key architect of the army's foreign policy of active neutrality. According to one political commentator, "Andrade speaks with leftist language, meets with the right, is an excellent intermediary between prominent military groups, and has important international connections."[14] He is regarded as a member of the "informed right."

The loss of Andrade further divided the party, which then nominated Jose Angel Lee Duarte in March 1990. Inter-party negotiations and intra-party squabbles intensified before the official campaign period starting in June 1990. Three other parties holding talks with the PSD and PR concerning party tickets were the United Revolutionary Front (FUR), Democratic Revolutionary Union (URD), and the United Guatemala Movement (MGU).

The Right

Most political parties in Guatemala are found on the right side of the political spectrum. They range from the National Liberation Movement (MLN), the longtime standard-bearer of anticommunist politics, to the National Centrist Union (UCN), which poses as a centrist party but leans decidedly to the right. In between are a jumble of other rightist parties that are commonly little more than platforms for their current leaders. As the 1990 elections approached, the right wing was marked by disunity and the absence of a clear vision of the future.

The right wing in Guatemala can be divided roughly into that part which is organized politically and that which is not. Suffering its worst crisis in 35 years, the organized right has found itself dangling without a popular base and out of touch with the political thinking of both the army and private sector. In a quandary of both ideology and organization, the right wing has found itself unable to adapt to the political changes brought on by the military-sponsored democratization process.

Since the late 1940s anticommunism, more visceral than rational, has been the driving force of the political right in Guatemala. The right wing has been characterized by its reactionary response — first to the Arévalo and Arbenz governments and later to all forms of popular dissidence — rather than by any coherent political program for change. Other elements historically included in the ideology shared by the political right have been its alliances with the Catholic church and with U.S. foreign policy.

In the era of *glasnost*, anticommunism as an ideology does not stir the blood of the party faithful as in the past. In the new political rhetoric adopted by the army and government, terrorism is posed as the main threat to democracy. But unlike the military, rightist parties have failed to modernize their political tactics. Like a defective phonograph needle, the extreme right remains stuck in its decades-old rut expounding on the communist threat to national security. Formerly at the center of power in Guatemala, the old political right now faces hard times. It finds itself on the outside of political and economic decision-making, left with only a few seats in the National Congress and conspiring on the sidelines with isolated factions of the military and oligarchy.

A major weakness of the right wing is its division into two sectors: political and economic. This division became apparent in the 1970s when a younger business class emerged which no longer identified with the antediluvian politics of the traditional oligarchy. Many of these new entrepreneurs embraced the economics of neoliberalism with its enshrinement of the free market and the private sector. Reflecting this trend, in 1971 the Francisco Marroquín University was founded to train the country's future economic power structure in the conservative principles of neoliberalism.

The adoption of the Chicago School's economics of free enterprise did not automatically find a home among the political right. For two decades, rightwing parties had played a part in the development of a corporativist state economic sector and had not objected as the military itself moved into the economic arena. It was, for example, during the MLN-PID government of Carlos Arana Osorio that the state increased its intervention in the economy through such public-sector corporations as INDECA, INAFOR, and BANDESA.

In Guatemala, although the economic right does not have its own political parties, it does boast powerful economic organizations, notably CACIF and to a lesser extent the Free Business Chamber (Cámara de Libre Empresa) and the Chamber of Business (CAEM).[15] By no means does the entire business elite fully share the faith in neoliberal economics. But the entire business community does share the conviction in the primacy of the business sector. This economic right — comprising both the neoliberal purists and the more pragmatic elements of CACIF — have had difficulty finding an appropriate electoral instrument within the political right.

In mid-1989 elements of the oligarchy formed the **National Unity Movement** with the intention of casting around to back one candidate that could win the election. The idea of this group and a subsequent one called the **Pyramid Group** was to select a candidate that represents the remodeled right wing, similar to Cristiani in El Salvador and Callejas in Costa Rica.[16]

The notorious old party of the extreme right, the **National Liberation Movement (MLN)** is directed by Mario Sandoval Alarcón, alleged godfather of the Central American death squads. As the party that led the coup that overthrew the Arbenz government, the MLN has long been looked on with favor by the traditional agroexport oligarchy and rightist factions within the military. Only once, however, has the MLN had a taste of political power. That was during the regime of Carlos Arana Osorio (1970-1974), who became president as part of a MLN-PID coalition. Since 1974 the MLN has waned but continues to serve as a base for the most extreme anticommunist political sentiments.

Under Cerezo, the debilitated MLN charged that the DCG government served as a front for international communism, asserting that the Cerezo government was fomenting social discontent as the first step in a civil war that would open up the country to communism. A member of the World Anti-Communist League (WACL), the MLN says that it is in the process of revitalizing the party but that it remains firm in its ideology: "Total and absolute unity against communism." Manuel Ayau, businessman and founder of the rightwing Francisco Marroquín University, was originally selected as the party's presidential candidate in 1990, but he withdrew apparently as part of negotiations to form a rightwing alliance. The MLN has toned down its violent and extremist rhetoric, mimicking the evolution of the ARENA party in El Salvador. During the peace talks with the URNG in Madrid in May 1990, Sandoval Alarcón surprised observers by adopting an extremely conciliatory and friendly position, apparently with an eye to broadening voter support for the MLN and the extreme right.

Founded in 1983 by *El Gráfico* publisher Jorge Carpio Nicolle, the **National Union Center (UCN)** is the country's second most powerful party, after the DCG. Benefiting from its ability to propagate publicity through the country's second-largest newspaper, the UCN quickly achieved the national prominence and outreach that other rightist parties lacked. Associated with the International Liberal Party based in Spain, the UCN poses publicly as a centrist party but is clearly in the rightwing political camp. It is characterized both by its political pragmatism and its rightwing populism. The party suffers from constant desertions and splinterings, usually over complaints that the party is little more than a vehicle for the personal political ambitions of Carpio Nicolle. The party suffered a major loss in 1988 with the departure of Ramiro de León Carpio, Jorge's cousin and key political adviser. Jorge Carpio Nicolle, while an adept politician, is not widely regarded as a statesman or intellectual.

The UCN faced a possible constitutional challenge to the Carpio Nicolle candidacy based on the fact that he could not legally take office in the event that his brother Roberto (who served as Cerezo's vice-president) became president due to the death or renunciation of Cerezo. Nonetheless, moving into the elections, it appeared to be the only party capable of presenting a serious challenge to the DCG. For a rightwing alliance to succeed, it would likely have to involve the UCN due to its position as the country's leading opposition party. In 1985, the UCN garnered 20 percent of the vote while all the other rightwing parties together accumulated only 27 percent of the vote (the DCG having won 39 percent).

In April 1990 the **Authentic Nationalist Central (CAN)**, an extreme right party that dates back to the Arana Osorio regime, announced that it was joining forces with the UCN for the 1990 elections. Until recently, the chief figure within this ultra-right party was Mario David García Velásquez, the director of the *Aquí El Mundo* television news program that was shut down by the Cerezo government for having promoted a coup attempt in May 1988. CAN backed the candidacy of García during the 1985 elections, during which the party managed to obtain one congressional seat. In the late 1980s CAN became a voice for the country's new set of neoliberals.

Founded in 1964 by chief-of-state Enrique Peralta Azurdia, the **Democratic Institutional Party (PID)** was known as the "army's party." PID's candidate, Aníbal Guevara, was the handpicked successor of Lucas García but he was replaced by a military coup within days of taking office in 1982. In 1985, in a political alliance with the MLN, the PID won one congressional seat. In the 1990 elections PID became the main supporter of the controversial candidacy of Ríos Montt, whose campaign slogan was "Security, Well-Being, and Justice." His reputation for moral rectitude and military firmness appealed to urban voters concerned about widespread corruption and increasing crime and political violence. Ríos Montt and his Alliance '90 campaign succeeded in building surprising support not only from Guatemalans attracted by his promise of law and order but also among neoliberals and sectors of the ultra-right and the army. His candidacy could also count on the backing of large sectors of the evangelical community. PID, the initial party sponsoring Ríos Montt, was the only political party that refused to attend talks with the URNG, reflecting the uncompromising position of General Ríos Montt.

As his candidacy continued to build, the National Election Board in August 1990 declined to register Ríos Montt as a legal candidate. The legal challenge to his candidacy focused on an article in the 1985 Constitution barring from the presidency those who have led a coup or armed revolution. His backers contended, however, that this prohibition could not be applied retroactively to him. Ríos Montt, called the "tropical Khomeini" by some, pledged to appeal the decision. Although some sectors of the army were supporting Ríos Montt, there were widespread fears that a Ríos Montt candidacy would spark a military coup by the same officers who ousted him in 1983. In the end, it will be the military which, as in most other affairs of government, will be the final arbiter of this and other election issues.

One of the newest rightwing parties, **Movement of Solidarity Action (MAS)** is a creation of Jorge Serrano Elías, a rightist evangelical who placed third in the 1985 presidential elections. Since its brief popularity in 1985, MAS has lost its political momentum. MAS is a member of the International Democrat Union, a conservative political association that includes the U.S. Republican Party.

Other rightwing groups include the **Guatemalan Nationalist Party (PANAG)**, led by Mario Castejón, ex-secretary general of the PNR, **National Unity Front (FUN)**, and the **National Advancement Plan Party (PAN)**, which is the personal organization of former Guatemala City mayor Alvaro Arzú. Arzú's candidacy counted on support among the business community in Guatemala City, but he is little-known outside the capital. His rightwing, private-sector politics did not prevent elements within the Christian Democratic Party from throwing their support to PAN at the outset of the campaign.

Not to be left out of the pre-election debate, a group of retired generals claimed that Guatemala needed a military candidate to reverse the country's deterioration. Proclaimed as the candidate of the newly formed **Emerging Movement of Harmony (MEC)** was General Benedicto Lucas, brother of General Romeo Lucas García. Among some military circles Benedicto Lucas, who served as chief of the military high command during his brother's regime (1978-1982), is highly regarded for his academic qualifications and for leading some of the army's strongest counterinsurgency offensives.

About 20 parties nominated candidates for the November 1990 elections. The beginning of the campaign was marked by a saturation of television and radio publicity, particularly by the DCG, PAN, UCN, MAS, and Ríos Montt's alliance. It was also distinguished by its absence of ideological debate and concrete political platforms. The floating of the *quetzal* and the conservative economic measures adopted by the government left the right wing with little ammunition for a strong ideological campaign. The DCG, in effect, had taken the wind out of the sails of the right wing. But by adopting the program of the right wing and ignoring popular demands the DCG had a more difficult time projecting itself as a centrist party.

The superficial nature of Guatemalan democratization became ever more apparent during the 1990 campaign. The political parties were based on personal ambitions rather than on ideas or their commitment to democracy. Despite the country's debilitated state, there was no substantial debate, at least in the early rounds, about the nation's economic direction, military control, or social reforms. Neither was there any link between the political parties and the rising chorus of demands from popular organizations.

Foreign Policy

Although not formally acknowledged, Guatemala's foreign relations have long been closely aligned with the United States. As the country's main investment and trading partner and its chief source of financial aid, the United States has maintained a large degree of economic and political hegemony over Guatemala. There exists a confluence of interests that has conditioned relations between the two nations. The United States is the country's main agroexport market, its main supplier of imports, and its principal supplier of investment capital. Especially since the mid-1950s, the United States has been Guatemala's principal partner in economic development, both in the agroexport sector and in the import-substitution industrial sector. Politically, both countries consider their national interests threatened by any serious rise in leftist popular opposition.

Although all these factors remained operative, tactical differences surfaced in the late 1970s. For the Carter administration, the stability of Guatemala could best be achieved by political and economic reforms and a cessation of gross human rights violations. The Guatemalan army saw the political situation differently. It contended that harsher emergency measures were needed to crush the rebellion. For this reason, Guatemala sought new sources of military aid mainly among other countries like Argentina, Israel, South Africa, and Taiwan.

Beginning in 1983 the policies of the two countries once again began to fall in line. Having successfully waged its campaign of counterinsurgency terror, the Guatemalan military was ready to pursue a strategy of economic and political stabilization. The military's program largely paralleled measures proposed by Washington, the European Economic Community, and the multilateral banks: transition from military to civilian rule, economic reactivation based on foreign aid, structural adjustment, and export promotion.

These new Guatemala initiatives dovetailed nicely with Washington's strategy of surrounding Nicaragua with U.S.-backed "democratic" republics. But while Guatemala's domestic policies closely matched the U.S. strategy for the region, the country's foreign policy did not find the same degree of acceptance in Washington.

Dubious Neutrality

For so long a pariah in the world of international relations, Guatemala adopted calculated measures in the early 1980s to improve its standing in the international community. From 1954 to 1983 the country had no formulated foreign policy. Neutrality began to emerge as the official foreign policy with Ríos Montt and took clearer form in late 1983 during the Mejía Víctores regime. The policy called for nonintervention in the internal affairs of other Central American nations and gave priority to resolving Guatemala's internal problems and its international isolation. The principal architect of the policy was Foreign Minister Fernando Andrade. The term "active neutrality" became popular with the Cerezo government.

"Active neutrality" is a foreign policy integrally associated with the military's search for "national stability."[17] Rather than offering unconditional support for the U.S. campaign of military and economic aggression against Nicaragua, Guatemala pursued a more neutral policy. Guatemala adopted this policy of active neutrality for three main reasons:

1. Resources were limited. There was a greater need to concentrate on the internal guerrilla challenge than to fight a regional war.

2. The country wished to enhance its international credibility and secure European assistance, which would be undermined by overt involvement in the U.S. anti-Sandinista agenda.

3. Any threat posed by Nicaragua, which does not share a border with Guatemala, was considered remote (in contrast with growing concern over the threat of revolutionary advance in El Salvador). A consensus was emerging that national economic stability was linked to peace in the region and the revival of regional trade.

Active neutrality also served the Guatemalan government and military by undermining the diplomatic influence of the URNG guerrillas while raising the diplomatic standing of the government. By ameliorating Guatemala's international position, the policy of active neutrality simultaneously reduced criticism of human rights violations, thereby freeing the military's hand in counterinsurgency operations.

Although active neutrality helped Guatemala improve its international image and prove its democratic credentials, it was a policy that was in practice not strictly followed. As relations improved with the United States, the Guatemalan military and civilian government began to provide covert aid for the Nicaraguan contras. According to a CIA memo, Guatemala agreed to provide clandestine logistical support and training for the contras in return for Washington's efforts to refurbish the country's international standing.[18] International arms shipments for the contras were channeled through the Guatemalan army, contras were trained at the Pólvora Special Counterinsurgency School in northern Petén, and the contras used Guatemala as a base for their political operations, which included a political training center established at the Francisco Marroquín University.[19]

Guatemala's involvement in armed conflict beyond its borders also extended to the civil war in El Salvador. During the guerrilla offensive of November 1989, an unspecified number of counterinsurgency specialists and advisers were sent to El Salvador, one of whom was held by Salvadoran guerrillas when they captured the Sheraton hotel in San Salvador.[20] Asked about this collaboration, Chief of Staff Manuel Callejas replied, "The Guatemalan army has always collaborated with the Salvadoran army, and that situation will not change."[21]

There have long been close relations between the extreme right in Guatemala, particularly the National Liberation Movement (MLN), and the rightwing ARENA party in El Salvador. This regional rightwing alliance may have been responsible for the death squad killing in January 1990 of Héctor Oquelí, secretary general of El Salvador's National Revolutionary Movement, and Gilda Flores, a lawyer associated with Guatemala's Democratic Socialist Party.

Through its active neutrality policy Guatemala was able to increase its international support. Even though it was a policy that was routinely violated, its public formulation and dissemination did serve to support the regional peace process. The policy did not, however, obstruct the expanding role of Washington in Guatemala. Within military and government circles, there is widespread recognition that continued national stability is largely contingent on domestic and foreign policies that correspond to the United States' own interests.

The Question of Belize

During the 1980s Guatemala moved towards normalized relations with Belize. Historically, Guatemalans have been educated to believe that Belize is part of their national territory. In fact, Belize still appears on maps as a department of Guatemala. However, beginning with "The Heads of Agreement" negotiations between the United Kingdom and Guatemala, acceptance of Belizean national sovereignty has grown. The establishment of a Permanent Joint Commission between Belize and Guatemala in May 1988 was a concrete sign of this progress, Guatemala having previously refused to negotiate directly with Belize. While still at issue is Guatemala's demand for land and water access to the Caribbean, only the extreme right wing in Guatemala clings to the notion that Belize will someday be a part of Guatemala.

The thawing of relations between the two countries reflects the military's efforts to guarantee the stability of its borders. This normalization is also an essential part of a foreign policy designed to broaden the country's range of diplomatic and economic contacts. An additional factor is a renewed interest in developing export markets in the Caribbean. Without normalized relations with Belize, the Caribbean Common Market (CARICOM) would remain closed to Guatemalan exporters.

The Peace Process

The Cerezo government initially played a key role in arranging regional talks among the five Central American presidents (Panama and Belize did not participate). Cerezo's ambitions to win international acclaim as a regional peacemaker were thwarted, however, by the more aggressive efforts of President Oscar Arias of Costa Rica. Revelations of Guatemala's support for the Nicaraguan contras and the superficial manner in which the Guatemala government implemented the peace accords contrasted sharply with Cerezo's professions of regional neutrality and commitment to peaceful solutions.

The provisions of the Esquipulas II peace accords, ratified by Guatemala in August 1987, were only superficially implemented within the country. In keeping with the accords, the Cerezo government did declare a political amnesty, but its main beneficiaries were military officers who participated in a May 1988 coup attempt against the government. Refugees returning from Mexico or displaced persons rounded up by the army have also been given amnesty but only after the military coerced them into signing amnesty declarations stating their repudiation of the guerrillas. Criticizing this use of amnesty, Americas Watch complained that "rather than opening a way for an individual to participate in political life, the acceptance of amnesty attaches to that individual the stigma of subversive association, which is extremely dangerous in Guatemala."[22] Other critics noted that amnesty was worthless unless the law also provided for the personal safety of those guerrillas who would turn themselves in.

As specified in the Esquipulas II peace accords, a national dialogue was initiated under the auspices of the newly established National Reconciliation Commission (CNR), which received strong support from the Catholic church. Representatives of the country's major political parties, churches, and popular organizations were represented in the CNR, but the relevance and impact of the CNR was undermined from the start by its failure to incorporate representatives of the URNG guerrilla coalition and groups of Guatemalan exiles who also petitioned for the right to participate. The failure of the military and the business coalition CACIF to join the dialogue also foiled the CNR's efforts to promote peace and justice.[23]

For all its limitations, the popular movement, represented by the Labor and Popular Action Union (UASP), regarded the national dialogue as an opportunity to raise their demands in a public forum sanctioned by the government. Dialogue participants and observers took advantage of the forum to establish links with each other and to forge a common strategy. The popular movement, however, approached the national dialogue mindful that past attempts to reach national accords over such issues as wages and human rights had been repeatedly sabotaged by other government agreements with the private sector and the army. Two popular sector representatives — delegates from the student and repatriated refugee communities — to the CNR were kidnapped and murdered.

Negotiations with the URNG

International pressure brought the Cerezo government to agree to discussions with URNG guerrilla coalition in October 1987, but this dialogue quickly lapsed due to rightwing reaction in Guatemala. URNG continued to express interest in reopening talks but was repeatedly rebuffed. It was not until early 1990 that a series of talks between the URNG and the country's political parties, private groups, and popular organizations was initiated. In March 1990 delegations from the URNG and CRN met in Oslo where it was decided that in a series of sessions sponsored by the CRN and the URNG would meet with the country's key economic, social, and political groups. The intent of these talks was to lay the foundation for direct negotiations between the rebels and the government and military.

Neither the government nor the military have indicated, however, that they would seriously consider a negotiated end to the conflict. It has been the government's unbending position that there can be no substantive talks until the guerrillas lay down their arms and incorporate themselves into the "democratic" process. The CNR also insisted that any accords reached with the URNG would have to be "within the limits of the constitution." For its part, the URNG insisted that any negotiated solution to the conflict will have to include measures that effectively address the country's underlying social and economic problems. The guerrilla leadership stated that it is not considering joining the electoral framework but is working toward the establishment of a "true democracy."

Human Rights

Extensive human rights violations have been a constant in Guatemala for almost four decades. As the intensity of popular organizing and guerrilla insurgency increases, the level of violations tends to increase. Rises in violations also commonly accompany pre-election campaigning. The country saw diminished human rights violations in the main urban centers during the short reign of Ríos Montt at the same time that massive terror ruled in the countryside. Following the 1986 inauguration of Vinicio Cerezo there was a marked reduction in the quantity of human rights violations. By the end of the decade, however, politically related deaths and disappearances had once again become an almost everyday occurrence.

Although human rights violations decreased after the height of the counterinsurgency war in the early 1980s, they remained at high levels by international standards. Even after Cerezo's inauguration, respected monitoring organizations like Amnesty International and Americas Watch continued to express grave concern about human rights violations on the part of the security forces. In 1988 the Council on Hemispheric Affairs placed Guatemala at the top of its list of Latin American countries with the most human rights violations. Americas Watch concluded in its 1988 report, "While the numbers of political killings are lower than in the early 1980s—a time of great carnage—the apparatus of state terror remains intact and undiminished in strength."[24]

The Cerezo government dismissed charges by international and local monitors of continuing human rights abuses. President Cerezo labeled the reports of continued disappearances "pure fiction," claiming that most are the result of family problems where children and fathers are running away to leave a bad "family situation."[25] The position of the Cerezo government that human rights conditions have markedly improved in the last three years of civilian government have been echoed by the U.S. State Department in its human rights reports.

For its part, the State Department until recently compared the human rights situation under the Cerezo government to that of the early 1980s, and noted that abuses had decreased. Its reporting also distinguished between the "government" and the "military," tacitly recognizing that the government had little control over the military. It noted that the government regularly condemns violations that do occur and that the judiciary is working to improve the investigation of these cases. The State Department also pointedly noted that the government itself is not to blame for the "infrequent" and "isolated" violations that do occur.

Among the conclusions of the 1988 State Department report were the following:

* "...there was no evidence that the government pursued a policy of political killing."
* "...reports of torture attributable to the military or police forces were infrequent."
* "There were no known cases in 1988 of persons being imprisoned for political reasons or for nonviolent exercise of basic human rights."
* "Members of the security forces work together in combined or coordinated operations to combat common crime and threats to national security....Changes in the judiciary and the police, as well as increased professionalism in the military, have had a positive impact on respect for human rights."[26]

The contention of the Cerezo government that it was doing all that it could to improve the human rights situation in Guatemala received certain support from a 1989 human rights assessment by the United Nations. The UN has declined to reclassify the country as a "worst offender" but voted to maintain a UN assessor in the country. This assessor concluded that "the violation of civil and political rights of Guatemalans is not the product of government policy, but the actions of powerful groups and can be linked to a climate of violence that still escapes control by the government."[27] In keeping with its pro-government tone, the report included only violations confirmed by the government and only the government's version of the Aguacate massacre of 22 peasants in November 1988.

While reported numbers do not tell the whole story about the human rights climate in Guatemala, they are an indication of the terror in which Guatemalans live. There was a sharp decline in the number of reported violations during the first year of Cerezo's term, but the situation steadily worsened afterwards. The May 1988 attempted coup marked the beginning of a period of rapidly increasing terror and repression in Guatemala.

In addition to killings and disappearances, human rights violations in Guatemala also involve arbitrary detentions, death threats, serious abuses of press freedom, maltreatment of prisoners, and the existence of civil patrols and model villages. In 1988, members of popular organizations and unions reported a rise in the frequency of death threats and arbitrary detention by security forces, designed, they say, to frighten activists into silence. In 1988 the offices of the liberal newsweekly *La Epoca*, the Soviet news agency Tass, and the Cuban news service Prensa Latina were all forced to close due to bombings and death threats.

A prison riot at the Pavón Rehabilitation Center brought attention to prison conditions: no windows, virtually no running water, no built-in electricity or heat, and food only once a day. The prison, built to house 1100, was holding twice that number, and many prisoners had been incarcerated for years without their relatives knowing anything about their location. Some had never been charged with a crime or brought before a judge.

While the horror of the human rights climate in Guatemala has long received international attention, it was not until recent years that human rights have been a publicly discussed issue within the country. Much credit for this goes to the Mutual Support Group (GAM), which despite the torture and disappearances of several of its own directors and members has persisted in denouncing abuses and demanding justice for past violations. The death of a GAM founder in 1985 was attributed by the army to a "lamentable accident." President Cerezo advised the group, 90 percent of whom are rural Indian women, to "stop acting macho" and "forget the past."

Other groups that have brought attention to human rights issues are National Coordinator of Guatemalan Widows (CONAVIGUA), Peace Brigades International, Runajel Junam Council of Ethnic Communities (CERJ), and Center for Investigation, Study, and Promotion of Human Rights (CIEPRODH). Besides denouncing human rights abuses, CERJ aims "to struggle to advance the goals of democracy, justice, and dignity of the Mayan peoples while fighting racial discrimination."

A 1989 Americas Watch report concluded that the country's three non-government human rights groups (CERJ, GAM, and CIEPRODH) have "a tenuous existence, operating in great isolation and a climate of tremendous insecurity." Furthermore:

Perhaps one of the greatest indicators of the depth of the repression in Guatemala has been the tragic history of efforts to establish human rights groups in Guatemala. Time and again, harassment, killings, disappearances, and the overwhelming fear they produce have thwarted the establishment of domestic monitoring groups. The absence of such groups, which could chronicle, investigate, and assign blame for the daily violations of the most fundamental rights, has worked to the tremendous advantage of successive Guatemalan regimes, allowing them to deny responsibility for innumerable tortured bodies found on countless roadsides.[28]

Government initiatives to investigate human rights violations have served more to polish the image of the government than to seriously address the issues. Four days before Cerezo's inauguration, the military passed an amnesty degree which exempted members of the security forces from prosecution for political or related common crimes. Cerezo supported this measure, but promised that he would become very "heavy-handed" if repression continued under his administration. Yet Cerezo's heavy hand has not been seen. During his tenure, no member of the security forces has been convicted and imprisoned for a politically motivated violent crime. The Human Rights Commission created by the Cerezo government was constrained by a low budget ($200 a month) and fear of accusing the military. In its first year, the commission received 900 denunciations of human rights violations but did little or nothing to investigate those cases.

The existence of the commission and the subsequent appointment of a Human Rights Prosecutor were cited by the Cerezo government as an example of its commitment to resolve the human rights problem. The government also repeatedly referred to the training that the Guatemalan judiciary received from Harvard Law School's Center for Criminal Justice to justify its claims that the government was working to improve the investigation and prosecution of political and common crimes. In television advertising, it claimed that the training program—funded by the U.S. Agency for International Development (AID)—was helping to correct the human rights situation in rural areas. According to Americas Watch, however, the judiciary has shown no inclination to prosecute cases of human rights violations. Furthermore, denunciations of human rights violations are passed from the Human Rights Commission to the Ministry of Defense or to the National Police, "in most cases, the same institutions from which the plaintiffs seek redress."[29]

By the fifth year of the Cerezo administration the deteriorating human rights climate was causing increasing problems for the government. The August 1989 assassinations of Christian Democratic leader Danilo Barillas and banker Ramiro Castillo — followed by a wave of disappearances and deaths of student leaders — signaled an escalation in the level of death squad terror and resulted in condemnations of the political violence from all quarters. Shocked by the Barillas and Castillo killings, private-sector leaders began to complain that the deepening climate of terror was undermining their ability to do business.

Accusations by the U.S. embassy in early 1990 that the government was doing little to clamp down on human rights abuses shocked the Cerezo administration. Throughout his term Cerezo had devoted considerable effort in international forums to shield Guatemala from condemnations of the country for its human rights abuses. The government and the military had been largely successful in blaming the increasing violations on the guerrillas, rightwing extremists, and narcotraffickers. But the State Department indicated that it was no longer accepting the official story. The January 1990 murder of Salvadoran socialist leader Héctor Oquelí and Guatemalan lawyer Gilda Flores of the Democratic Socialist Party sparked strong international rebuke for the country's human rights climate. The case was immediately compared to the massacre of six Jesuit priests in El Salvador two months before. Americas Watch observed that if the U.S. government were "consistent with its own report," it would immediately cut military aid to Guatemala.[30]

Chapter 2

Military

Security Forces

The Guatemalan armed forces — incorporating the accumulated wisdom and experience of U.S., Israeli, Taiwanese, and Argentine advisers — seriously set back the guerrilla insurgency of the early 1980s with ruthless violence and sophisticated pacification techniques. Not only did the Guatemalan army demonstrated a remarkable ability to combine "security" and "development" in its counterinsurgency efforts, but it also successfully carried out a nation-building project that further strengthened the state against subversion. Notably, the military conducted this multifaceted campaign without large infusions of foreign assistance — in marked contrast to neighboring El Salvador.

As successful as counterinsurgency in Guatemala has been and as invincible as the military may appear, the stability and security of the Guatemalan state remain precarious for the following reasons:

* Despite massive butchering of dissidents and the militarization of society, the army has failed over the last three decades to rid the country of the guerrilla threat. Its recent claims to have finished off the guerrillas have proved to be wishful thinking. By the late 1980s the guerrilla movement was once again seriously challenging the power of the military at the same time that the popular movement was gaining new strength and visibility. National security, as defined by the army and its advisers, seems to be an unachievable goal. As a result, counterinsurgency has become a permanent state of affairs.

* The army's apparent success in gaining control over the rural population is related more to its use of terror than to the performance of its civic-action and psychological-operations teams. Since 1954 the security forces have eliminated successive generations of community leaders, activists, and educators, leaving communities largely unorganized and deprived of social and

political foundations. But the resulting void in popular political
education and experience has not meant that the army and
government have been able to shape the kind of supportive social
base necessary for national stability. Nor has this constant
repression succeeded in keeping a lid on popular organizing.

* Counterinsurgency theorists generally recognize that deteriorating
socioeconomic conditions create a base for insurgency. Despite a
widespread commitment within the military for a developmentalist
side of counterinsurgency, it has been unable to conceptualize and
implement the kind of development projects that would indeed
alter the socioeconomic circumstances of the countryside. Instead,
the development component of counterinsurgency has been
translated into welfare-type projects that depend on the continued
flow of supplies and funds from foreign governmental and
nongovernmental donors.

* The military high command has guided a nation-building project
designed to create a modernized state capable of responding
politically, socially, and economically to revolutionary insurgence.
Although successful in establishing the structure of a modern state,
the army's nation-building efforts have failed as yet to cement the
kind of national-unity pact needed to support its broad vision of
counterinsurgency. The key sectors that would be included in such a
pact — the Catholic church, worker and peasant organizations, the
business community, and the political parties — have each refused,
for differing reasons, to offer the required support. Even significant
elements within the armed forces have rejected the modernization
vision and "state stability" model backed by the military high
command.

* Continued repression and military control of the civilian
government have undermined the government's credibility and
dashed hopes that political modernization would bring peace,
stability, and progress. As public enthusiasm for the
"democratization" process has waned, the potential for widespread
social turmoil and armed rebellion has increased.

* The capacity of the military to wage an offensive war has been
increasingly undermined by it lack of funds, supplies, and
equipment, particularly aircraft.

Although the scorched-earth tactics of the military's counterinsurgency offensive in the early 1980s did undermine the strength of the URNG
guerrillas, the tenacity of the armed resistance has consistently con-

founded army predictions of their imminent demise. In the late 1980s, in fact, the guerrillas exhibited increasing resiliency and determination, both militarily and diplomatically. The army's attempts to finish off URNG on these two fronts have failed.

At the start of the 1990s the army finds itself without a firm source of international support. Washington has provided a wide range of support given the congressional limitations on direct military aid, but the Guatemalan army had counted on more. The precarious state of the economy and government finances make it difficult for the military to extract funds to re-equip or mount offensives. Although the Pentagon has supplied some logistical and material support, the Guatemalan military has been unable to maintain a strong air capacity, which is critical for offensives in the isolated jungle and mountain areas where the guerrillas maintain their bases. In the last couple of years the URNG has improved its capabilities to shoot down army helicopters, thus further limiting the strength of the military's air force.

Structure of the Armed Forces

There are three armed forces in Guatemala: Army, Navy, and Air Force. The Army, with some 43,000 troops, is the dominant element in this tripartite defense structure. In contrast, the Navy has only 1,200 members (including 600 marines) and the Air Force counts on only 850 (including 500 conscripts). Thus in Guatemala the Army is largely synonymous with the entire military.

The High Command (Estado Mayor) is the strategic command of the Army, the dominant element in the armed forces. It is here that the politics and overall strategy of the armed forces are developed. Under the High Command come the tactical commands: Personnel, Intelligence, Operations, Logistics, and Civil Affairs. The commands of the Navy and the Air Force are not included within these divisions but fall under the jurisdiction of the army zone commanders, despite their national focus.

In the last few years, the army has mounted a nationwide publicity campaign about the values of military service. Officially, military service is the duty of all Guatemalan males. In fact, men trying to obtain a passport must show their military enlistment card. But universal military service is a myth, as is voluntary recruitment. Generally, only the sons of the rural poor serve in the ranks of the army. They are, for the most part, recruited forcibly. Typically, army trucks arrive in a village on market days and the feast days of patron saints with the local military commissioner signaling which youth should be recruited. The forcible roundup of over 900 poor urban youth during an unprecedented "recruiting" campaign by military commissioners was defended by the army as its "normal practice."

With the reduced intensity of the counterinsurgency war after 1983 and the widening economic crisis, some rural youth have voluntarily enlisted, attracted by the $35 monthly pay and another $20 for their parents. Good food, shelter, and military privileges have also increasingly attracted poor Guatemalan youth. Officers come generally from middle-class *ladino* stock. To the rank of colonel, promotions are tied to tenure and performance, having little to do with personal connections.

Among the most important military institutions are the following:

* *Polytechnical School:* This is the officer training school (like West Point) from which students graduate with the rank of sub-lieutenant.

* *School of Military Studies (CEM):* Officers (majors and above) receive advanced training here.

* *Military Social Welfare Institute (IPM):* Officially, IPM is the military's pension and investment fund, but unofficially it is a source of capital for investments both on the part of the armed forces and individual officers. This tax-exempt corporation manages numerous economic concerns, including the army commissary, an insurance company, a multi-level parking lot in the center of Guatemala City, and several urban properties. IPM's most lucrative concern is the Army Bank, which it created in 1972.[1]

* *Army Bank:* The nation's tenth-largest bank, capitalized by the IPM and tax revenues, has military officers as its major stockholders and advertises that it provides "the safest place for your money."

* *Adolfo Hall:* This is a secondary school known for its military-style education. Not all graduates, however, enroll in the armed forces; many parents send their children to Adolfo Hall for its disciplinary reputation.

The Privatization of the Military

For the last fifteen years, the Guatemalan armed forces have become increasingly integrated into the private sector and the national oligarchy. The trend, which began with the Arana regime in 1970, has been called the "Somocization of Guatemala," referring to the way the Somoza family used its control of the National Guard for personal and political benefit. Anastasio Somoza, in fact, is said to have personally advised Arana about how to go about acquiring wealth. It used to be that the army was considered to be the *"cholero de la burguesía"* (half-breed servant of the wealthy). While there are still elements of this relationship, the military and its officers now have economic power and respect in their own right.

The Military Social Welfare Institute (IPM) and the Army Bank are the center of this new-found financial status, but the tentacles of martial economic power extend to all sectors of the economy and into the most isolated regions of Guatemala. Since the 1970s, the centers of economic aggrandizement for colonels and generals have been the Northern Transverse Strip, the Petén territory, and the department of Alta Verapaz. It became common practice during the Arana, Laugerud, and Lucas García regimes for high-ranking officers to receive large plots of land in the frontier regions slated for peasant colonization projects.[2]

Among the public-sector corporations that fell under military control in the 1970s and early 1980s were INDE (National Electrification Institute), Aviateca national airline, Aurora international airport, GUATEL (national telephone company), and Channel 5 television station. In addition, the military controls such state agencies as the National Reconstruction Committee (CRN), National Emergency Committee (CONE), National Geographic Institute, and FYDEP (Petén development directorate which is now being dismantled).

Active and retired military officers have moved in and out of these corporations and agencies always in the name of making them more efficient and accountable, but inevitably advancing them to new levels of corruption. Military corruption, while no longer at the exorbitant levels seen during the Lucas García regime, continues to be a fact of life in Guatemala, ranging from cases of major graft to low-level plundering, such as vehicle-importing deals and other customs fraud. The army's past record of intervening in the economy and in the administration of public services supposedly for the public good undermines the credibility, especially among the private sector, of the army's current nation-building projects. Another dimension of the military's broad power is the small weapons industry it operates, including an armored-vehicle plant in Santa Ana Berlín and a munitions factory in Cobán.

The Soft Sell

Since the April 1982 release of the National Security and Development Plan, the military has been committed to pursuing what could be called the "soft" side of counterinsurgency. This is not to say that the army has shirked from military offensives designed to defeat the insurgency while keeping the rural population terrified and passive. Massacres, torture, random terror, and aerial bombardments continue as part of a campaign to guarantee national security. These "hard" tactics, however, are now usually combined with measures designed to pacify, to some degree, the guerrillas' rural base of support. As the military began to gain a firmer hold on the conflictive highlands in 1982 and 1983, this other side of counterinsurgency received increasing attention. The various aspects of this soft sell of national security include:

* Pacification of the population in conflictive zones through civic-action projects, model villages, re-education and psychological operations, food distribution, and development projects.

* Modernization of the Guatemalan state through a process of "democratization."

* Limited reforms designed to broaden the financial base of government (tax increases) and pacify popular organizations (wage hikes, land sales programs, increased social services).

The Civil Affairs command is responsible for the pacification efforts. Civil Affairs, created as a military command in 1982, is an outgrowth of the army's civic-action programming, formerly a branch of the intelligence command. Civic action and nation-building have been components of military operations since the early 1960s, when the U.S. army began civic-action training and activities in Guatemala in response to the birth of an armed resistance. Guatemala, in fact, was the first Latin American country to receive this kind of military assistance from the United States.

There is a Civil Affairs section (S-5) associated with each of the 19 military zones, although the focus of Civil Affairs operations is the conflictive zones. According to the army, S-5 teams "act as advisors to the Military Zone Commanders on the political, economic, social, and social-psychological aspects of military operations." These teams are composed of soldiers specially trained in the areas of social services, psychological techniques, and ideological indoctrination. Usually nonuniformed, they function as a fifth column for the military in conflictive zones. Their work includes: intelligence gathering, re-education of the displaced and refugees, coordination of the projects of government ministries in targeted zones, and, in general, implementation of the "development" side of counterinsurgency.

In addition to coordinating development, Civil Affairs also manages the army's extensive psychological operations. It is called upon to "create an efficient leadership, which permits the formation of local leaders to spread the doctrinal elements of counterinsurgency strategy. The leadership must incorporate social promotion and community organization to arrive at integral community development."[3]

Saving the Nation

The Guatemalan army not only prides itself on protecting the country from communists but has also assumed the "historic task of saving the nation:"

> At the present time, we consider ourselves to be...the institution which gives impetus to democracy....We defend the interests of the nation in their totality...through political and military action encompassing all the nation, a military action which has reciprocal actions in the economic, political, and social fields.

With itself in the vanguard of this nation-saving project, the military has called upon all sectors to participate "within an integrated concept of the Guatemalan State." Closely related to this integrated nation-building project was a recent military initiative in the area of political strategy embodied in the September 1988 creation of the Center for Strategic Studies for National Stability (ESTNA). According to then Defense Minister General Hector Alejandro Gramajo, the objective of ESTNA is to "promote better understanding among the different elements of Guatemala's leadership circles, and to give these leaders a better understanding of the global strategic concept the army has conceived as the most adequate for the current situation in Guatemala."

ESTNA is aimed at building a consensus for the state, as conceived by the army and its civilian advisors, and at creating a political establishment which will defend that conception of the state. Although clearly a military institution, ESTNA is directed by and receives its financing from the military-spawned Foundation for the Institutional Development of Guatemala (DIG), a nongovernmental organization (NGO) whose board of directors includes both civilian and military members (including Gramajo himself). As an NGO, DIG can attract international funding that could not be granted directly to a government or military project. ESTNA is but one element in the military high command's efforts to establish a common definition of national stability. General Juan Leonel Bolaños, then vice-chair of Defense Chiefs of Staff, described the process this way:

> To counteract the occurrence of those elements which oppose the strategy of the military and other centers of power, the Guatemalan Army deems necessary the establishment of an educational process oriented towards all strata in the nation, with the object of learning to live within a system of democratic life and maintaining in this manner the constitutional order.[4]

In May 1990 Defense Minister Gramajo, the architect of the army's "state stability" model, retired and was replaced by his protégé General Juan Leonel Bolaños. Although Bolaños apparently shares Gramajo's political vision, he is regarded to be less capable and sophisticated than his predecessor. Named as assistant Army Chief of Staff was General Roberto Matta Galvez, who has also been mentioned as a future Minister of Defense. Matta, close to the Christian Democrats, has the reputation of being more a military hardliner than either Gramajo or Bolaños.

Splits within the Military

The Guatemalan armed forces have long been torn by tactical differences and divisions between the ranks. A long-running source of tensions has been the split between those favoring developmental and nation-building programs and those committed to a strictly military approach to maintaining national stability. The Committee for National Reconstruction (CRN), created in 1976, was, for example, largely a project of the army developmentalists. In early 1980s the adoption of the National Plan for Security and Development (PSND) represented a fusion of the two approaches to counterinsurgency and a moderation of tensions between the two camps. But as the guerrillas began to recuperate their former strength and the civilian government became less capable of forging a national consensus, earlier differences between the reformist and hardline approach began to resurface.

The unity of the Guatemalan military has also been weakened at times by splits between junior and senior officers. The military crisis of 1983 aggravated this division resulting in the coup by younger officers led by Efraín Ríos Montt. This fractioning became apparent again in the late 1980s as the younger officers who were on the frontlines of the counterinsurgency war grew increasingly frustrated with the military high command which was directing the war. They resented the luxuries available to these senior officers who were not directly involved in the increasingly dangerous counterinsurgency campaigns. In many cases, the internal divisions in the military assume an ideological form when in fact the dispute has more to do with the division of privileges and perks.[5]

Since the switch to civilian rule the army has been wracked by a split over the best strategy for ensuring national security and stability. While Defense Minister Gramajo insisted that the maintenance of the democratization process is the best way to defeat the leftist insurgency and to ensure economic stability, hardliners contended that the political opening has grown dangerously wide and that the more repressive tactics of the pre-1982 years need to be reinstituted.

In May 1987 a military faction, calling itself the "Officers of the Mountain," began publishing clandestine communiques critically analyzing the government and the Gramajo faction. These internal critics represented the most rightwing elements within the army, most being veterans of the 1978-1983 counterinsurgency war. Many, in fact, were still commanding troops involved in counterinsurgency efforts. Their dissatisfaction had both economic and political dimensions. The emergence of the "Officers of the Mountain" faction also reflected a long-standing rift between field commanders and desk officers.

The Officers of the Mountain challenged Gramajo's contention that the counterinsurgency war had been reduced to a police action against isolated bands of terrorists. From their battlefront perspective, these military dissidents knew that the guerrilla offensive was still causing large numbers of casualties. The re-emergence of the CUC peasant group and the presence in the country of opposition figure Rigoberta Menchú irked the Officers of the Mountain who felt that the fighting forces were getting the short shrift in this pretentious new democracy. While members of the high command and officers in the city were living high, the dissidents charged that the combatants were not getting the aid they needed to fight the war successfully.

Limited at first to grumbling in the barracks, the internal tensions exploded into the open on May 11, 1988. Dissident officers, supported by ultra-right political parties and sectors of the oligarchy, attempted a coup. Among the immediate factors that precipitated this break in the ranks were the following:

* The August 1987 signing of the Esquipulas II peace accords which required negotiations with the URNG and the beginning of a national dialogue.

* The November 1987 meeting in Madrid between government and URNG representatives.

* The embarrassing failure of the "Year's End" offensive in late 1987, which was finally called off in March 1988 after major casualties and an obvious failure to stamp out the tenacious guerrilla forces. The effort, which involved over 6,000 military combatants, was called the "final battle against the insurgency" by General Gramajo, but it ended without even so much as a final report.

* A March 1988 government pact with the UASP popular coalition that the oligarchy and rightwing officers regarded as a compromise with leftists.

* The arrival in the country in April 1988 of a Unity Representation of the Guatemalan Opposition (RUOG) delegation, a commission of political opponents closely associated with the URNG.
* The success of the Christian Democratic Party and the rout of the rightwing parties in the April 1988 municipal elections, which signaled to the country's hardliners the futility of the electoral option as a path to power.
* The failure of the government and military high command to secure substantially higher levels of military aid from the United States.

For the backers of the May 1988 and subsequent coup attempts (August 1988 and May 1989), the political and military situation had gotten out of hand. While always ideologically opposed to the foreign policy of "active neutrality" owing to their support of the contras, this opposition crescendoed to new levels as it became apparent the Esquipulas peace accords were having repercussions at home. URNG took full advantage of this political opening to the chagrin of the government, the military, and the oligarchy. Not only was URNG strong on the diplomatic front, but it also showed increased vitality and durability on the battlefield.

Although not taking full responsibility for the various 1988-1989 coup attempts, the clandestine Officers of the Mountain were certainly among the rebel ranks. The coups appeared to be negotiating maneuvers rather than serious attempts to seize state power. However these intrigues did not succeed in breaking the alliance between the Cerezo government and the military high command. In fact, the coup attempts had the result of rendering the civilian government yet more dependent on the Gramajo faction. While Cerezo and Gramajo survived the rebellions, many of the demands of the rebel officers were respected, including: the cancellation of the agreement with UASP, the closing of the political opening for URNG, increased spending for military supplies, the reinsertion of military officers into key positions in the public administration, increased military control over police forces, and maintenance of civil patrols.

The Officers of the Mountains and other rightwing elements within the armed forces have received direct backing and encouragement from ultra-right political and economic factions. Significantly, the coup attempts and threats of 1988-1989 were not condemned by the leading voices of the private sector. Instead, the destabilizing impact of the attempted coups served the immediate interests of the private sector in that both the government and the army hardened their position against popular demands for wage increases and price freezes.

The maneuverings of the Officers of the Mountains and the degree to which coup-mongering was accepted by the private sector demonstrates just how fragile and unsubstantial the democratization process really is. It became apparent that sizable factions of the military and the private sector were not prepared to accept the full significance of the "institutional re-encounter" as outlined by the military's leading political strategists.

In the late 1980s the military tightened its links with the Pentagon and U.S. suppliers, a direction firmly supported by Defense Minister Gramajo. The army, for example, was rearmed with U.S.-manufactured weapons. That U.S. aid has never risen to the levels first expected has generated concern and tensions within the military. A complete halt to U.S. support would severely debilitate the army and might lead to serious institutional instability, given the difficulty of finding other sources of external support.

The candidacy of Ríos Montt has raised the possibility of new splits within the military. Although there are clearly elements within the military that would like to see the retired general serve as president again, there are others who regard Ríos Montt as a destabilizing element who could spark increased guerrilla activity and increase social and political tensions.

Civil Patrols

Civil patrols have been the army's main instrument in maintaining the militarization of the Guatemalan countryside. The Civilian Defense Patrols (PAC), which were first formed in Alta Verapaz in 1976 and expanded in mid-1981 by the Lucas regime, became a central element in the counterinsurgency strategy of the Ríos Montt government aimed at breaking guerrilla links with the population. By late 1984 there were more than 900,000 members of the civil patrol system.

Supposedly a voluntary movement, the civil patrols were in truth obligatory. All males above 16 years were required to "volunteer" several days a week to serve in these military-directed patrols. Failure to volunteer meant being branded a guerrilla sympathizer and often resulted in imprisonment and torture at the local army base. Beginning in 1982 civil patrols became an ubiquitous part of rural life. At every entrance to most villages, civil patrols maintained guard posts to monitor the movement of visitors and villagers alike. According to a 1985 army publication describing its rural pacification strategy, the civil patrols "have doubled the efficiency of the security forces in creating the conditions of peace basic to the integrated development of these communities."[6]

Although civil patrols are no longer as extensive and numerous as they were in the early 1980s, they remain an important element in the military's counterinsurgency operations in the most conflictive zones. In some communities, they function as paramilitary squads that terrorize the local population. In army offensives in the highlands, civil patrols are ordered to seek out and destroy settlements of displaced families associated with the Communities of Population in Resistance (CPR) and to enter into direct conflict with guerrilla units. The disbandment of the civil patrols is one of the major demands of the country's human rights groups and campesino associations. The right wing and the army, however, are calling for the extension of the civil patrol system into the cities, where guerrillas have mounted new anti-military actions.

As a candidate, President Cerezo promised to abolish the patrols, charging that defense was the responsibility of the military not the civilian population. The failure to disband the patrols sparked the formation of a daring popular organization called the Runajel Junam Council of Ethnic Communities (CERJ), which means "all are equal" in the Quiché dialect. Since 1988 this Santa Cruz del Quiché group has called for an end to the civil patrol system, later renamed the Voluntary Committees of Civil Defense. CERJ, which has condemned the civil patrols as a form of military conscription, calls upon the rural male population to exercise their constitutional rights not to serve in what is the most extensive civil-patrol network in the world.

Although the military disbanded patrols in areas no longer considered conflictive, the patrols remain a central part of village life in many other areas. Considering the patrols an essential part of its efforts to maintain control over rural areas, the military has lashed back at CERJ with repression and widespread psychological operations. Four members of CERJ were disappeared in April 1989, and CERJ's director, Amilcar Méndez, has been the target of repeated death threats. The army has also employed the techniques of psychological warfare to discredit CERJ. Civil Affairs teams show videotapes in which CERJ is denounced as a guerrilla front. These tapes also include bloody footage from the Vietnam war with warnings that such terror could befall Guatemala if Indian villagers do not join the civil patrols. The civil patrols have themselves been used to attack popular organizations such as CERJ and GAM. In November 1988 a Catholic priest was run out of a village in southern Quiché by member of the civil patrol who charged him and members of Catholic Action with supporting the guerrillas.

The main function of the civil patrols is population control, functioning as the eyes and ears of the military. The patrols also fulfill a certain political or administrative role which has been superimposed by the army over traditional community organizational structure. In the most conflictive areas the civil patrols serve as combat auxiliaries, often accompanying the army in military sweeps and capturing displaced families eluding military control. The patrols also fulfill a propaganda function by spreading an anti-leftist message among their communities and accusing those who resist joining the patrols of being pro-guerrilla.[7]

After a dramatic reduction in the patrol system during the early years of the Cerezo administration, the patrols increased again in the late 1980s. In early 1990 the army said there were 450,000 patrol members while other estimates were as high as 600,000. Rightwing parties and elements within the army have suggested that the system be extended to the cities, particularly in the light of increased urban activity by the URNG.

The Army and the Displaced

A lingering problem in the military's efforts to maintain close control over the rural population has been the plight of refugees and displaced persons. It has attempted to deal with this problem by:

* Mounting offensives, including extensive use of civil patrols, to round up groups of displaced peasants living in the mountains beyond military supervision. Once collected, this displaced population is placed under military custody and subjected to "re-education" courses conducted by Civil Affairs officers. The army relies on foreign assistance, mainly from the World Food Program and the European Economic Community (EEC), and local NGOs to provide for the material needs of this captive population.

* Distributing land through the government's Institute for Agrarian Transformation (INTA) to those returned refugees and displaced persons considered most likely to resist guerrilla advances. This redistributed land generally belongs to refugees living in Mexico or to those displaced communities still living secretively and fearfully in the mountains.

* Directing foreign-funded development projects to strategic areas, particularly the Ixil Triangle and the Ixcán, in line with earlier plans for development poles.

* Closely monitoring the focus and activity of the government's Special Commission for the Repatriated and the Displaced (CEAR).

Police Divisions

Under the Cerezo government, the police forces were strengthened and re-equipped. At first, it appeared that the new civilian government would exercise a tighter reign on the country's various police forces. But throughout the 1980s the police continued to operate above the law and under military control. As with the military, no members of the Guatemalan police have ever been brought to trial for human rights violations.

Immediately after taking office, President Cerezo disbanded the notorious 600-member Department for Technical Investigations (DIT), a judicial police unit implicated in political violence. Yet the move amounted to little more than public relations as some four hundred of the DIT police were incorporated into the National Police and DIT was soon reconstituted as the Special Investigations and Narcotics Brigade (BIEN). More recently BIEN was renamed the Department for Criminal Investigations (DIC), which receives assistance and training from the U.S. Justice Department. According to an Americas Watch report, the DIC is infiltrated by army intelligence (G-2) agents and, like its predecessor DIT, remains subordinate to the military.[8]

The National Police, with 9,500 members, is the principal police organization. The Treasury Police (Guardia de Hacienda), with 2,100 members, though not as large as the National Police, enhances its influence by closely working with the army's G-2 intelligence command.

Under the Cerezo government the National Police was the favored recipient of considerable foreign training and supplies from the United States, Spain, West Germany, and other European countries. This aid raised concerns among sectors of the military that the Cerezo government was creating a source of armed power independent of the military. Under the jurisdiction of the Ministry of Government there was also considerable frustration that the police were receiving new equipment and vehicles at a time when the army itself sorely needed re-equipping. This conflict was resolved at least temporarily following the May 1988 coup attempt when the government agreed both to increase efforts to resupply the military and to cede control over the National Police to the military. The militarization of the police deepened in 1989 when an army general replaced a civilian as Minister of Justice.

The creation of SIPROCI (Civil Protection System) in 1988 also allayed fears that the government was crossing over into the security business. This new police unit, placed directly under the army's high command, coordinates the Mobile Military Police (PAM), civil patrols, National Police, and Treasury Police. Aside from asserting military control over the country's various police forces, SIPROCI was apparently created in an effort to avoid internecine conflicts between the various units. Its formation came in the wake of an ongoing dispute between the National Police and the Treasury over an incident in which the National Police arrested members of the Treasury Police who were linked to death squad killings.

One stated objective of SIPROCI is to present a common police front to rising street crime in Guatemala City. As it turns out, the new SIPROCI coordinated units did little to reduce the crime wave but has proved effective in breaking strikes and removing workers from occupied workplaces.

Paramilitary Groups

Although most death squad activity is directly sponsored by the security forces, the country also has a history of private rightwing paramilitary squads. Military-sanctioned paramilitary violence was responsible for much of the repression inflicted on the left and the popular movement arising from the 1954 coup. A second surge of paramilitary violence, coordinated largely by the National Liberation Movement (MLN), arose as part of the counterinsurgency campaigns of the 1960s. The two major death squads of this period were the White Hand and the New Anti-Communist Organization. Some sources report that death squads killed between 30,000 and 40,000 people during the 1966-1973 period.[9]

Paramilitary killings and disappearances rose again in the late 1970s and early 1980s. In 1983, with the incorporation of the civil patrol system, the armed forces counted on a new dimension of paramilitary activity. Death squad violence did decrease during the first year of the Cerezo administration but increased dramatically by the end of the decade. At first Cerezo and the military high command blamed the rise in disappearances and killings on common criminals and leftist terrorists. By the turn of the decade, however, both the government and the military charged that rightwing extremists and narcoterrorists were behind the scourge of death squad killings of student leaders, politicians, and community activists. International human rights groups and even the U.S. ambassador charged that the government was doing little or nothing to control the paramilitary violence and was to some degree implicated itself in the rash of murders and disappearances of the 1988-1989 period.

With the incorporation of the civil patrols (PAC) in 1983, the military organized a system of paramilitary activity involving as many as 900,000 men and boys. While death squad activity remained an undercurrent of life in Guatemala, it was not until 1988 that death squads again began publicly identifying themselves. In May 1988, while dissident elements in the military were mounting a coup attempt, the White Hand took credit for death threats to a Cuban correspondent for Prensa Latina, while the Secret Anti-Communist Army (ESA) claimed responsibility for firebombing the home of the Tass correspondent. In 1989, a new death squad known as Jaguar of Justice (JJ) emerged. "We will bring to justice thieves, murderers, youth gang members, child abusers, corrupt bureaucrats, and political gangsters — both left and right," pledged JJ in its first press release.

According to the Cerezo government, "No death squad exists in the country. We live in a legal regime and the security forces act democratically in accordance with the law."

The army's Presidential Department of Communications, located next to the National Palace, has long been considered one of the most important links between the military and paramilitary activities. The army's Intelligence (G-2) agents, who work closely with the National Police and the Department for Criminal Investigations (DIC), are regarded as directly responsible for death squad operations.

Guerrilla Opposition

Guatemala has the longest-running guerrilla opposition in Latin America. The origins of guerrilla warfare can be traced to a failed coup in 1960 by a group of reformist officers angry with government corruption and the use of Guatemalan territory to train Cuban exiles for the Bay of Pigs invasion. The rebel officers fled the country but returned in early 1962 to begin guerrilla warfare and were joined by revolutionaries from the Guatemalan Communist Party. This guerrilla effort was quickly crushed but its survivors regrouped in late 1962 to form the Rebel Armed Forces (FAR), which harassed the army until 1969 when its hardpressed remnants straggled into exile in Mexico.

After a period of reflection and analysis, two new guerrilla organizations — Guerrilla Army of the Poor (EGP) and the Organization of People in Arms (ORPA) — emerged in the 1970s and were later joined by FAR. Unlike the 1960s, when the emphasis was on forming "*focos*" or centers of guerrilla operation that would ignite widespread revolutionary war, the new guerrilla fronts place more emphasis on popular education and the political formation of peasant communities.

This new strategy proved successful in mobilizing widespread support for revolutionary objectives. But the newly formed guerrilla armies were neither sufficiently organized nor prepared for the terror that descended upon them and upon the communities where they were working (mainly in the villages of the northwestern highlands, the FTN, and the Petén). While they met their popular education objectives, the revolutionary forces had not advanced to the stage where they were able to incorporate large numbers of peasants into guerrilla units. Nor were they strong enough to defend the Indian communities from the army's wholesale butchering.

The counterinsurgency war, which reached its height from 1981 through 1983, crushed the unarmed resistance movement and seriously weakened the guerrilla forces themselves. The brunt of the 1981-1983 war was aimed at destroying or disarticulating the guerrillas' unarmed rural support base. This campaign came on the heels of several years of intensive repression against popular organizations, development groups, and community organizations, in both rural and urban areas.

Though the guerrilla armies survived, they could no longer count on ample bases of popular support. The army had clearly made its point: any support for the "terrorists" would be dealt with in the cruelest fashion, which often meant eliminating entire villages. While fear was certainly the main factor in breaking the strong links between the guerrillas and Indian communities, disillusionment, fed by army propaganda, also contributed to diminishing revolutionary sentiment. Many felt that the guerrillas had promised more than they could deliver and had failed to protect them when violence struck. The army's developmentalist and democratization strategies also isolated the guerrilla armies. Instead of news of massacres and burning villages, military-sponsored food distribution programs and the electoral process came to dominate international headlines.

Who They Are and What They Want

Since 1982 four guerrilla forces have been united in the Guatemalan National Revolutionary Unity (URNG), which functions as both the diplomatic and military command of the armed revolutionary movement. While Marxism-Leninism has been the dominant ideological tendency within URNG, there are also strong liberation-theology and social-democratic tendencies. Depending on the guerrilla army, the combatants are largely Indian and many have joined the armed struggle because of their Christian perspective.

The four guerrilla armies that compose URNG often operate under common field commands and in some cases have mounted joint operations. They are, however, distinguished by different geographical areas of concentration and varying political philosophies. The EGP, which established itself in the highlands in 1972, operates mainly in northern Quiché and Huehuetenango. Its commander is Rolando Morán. FAR, the oldest guerrilla army, concentrates on the south coast and the Petén, although it is also active in the highlands. The commander of FAR is Pablo Monsanto. ORPA began operations in 1972, and, after years of education and organizing, launched its first military operation in 1979. Its base is found in Sololá, San Marcos, and Quezaltenango, and to a much lesser extent in Chimaltenango, and Totonicapán. Its commander is Rodrigo Asturias (also known as Gaspar Ilom), son of the famous Guatemalan novelist Miguel Angel Asturias who wrote *Men of Corn* and *El Señor Presidente*. The fourth component of URNG is the PGT Central Committee which joined the guerrilla coalition in early 1989.

The five main points of URNG's 1982 revolutionary platform are the following:

1. Elimination of repression and guarantees of life and peace.

2. Distribution of property of the very wealthy, agrarian reform, price controls, and the allowance of reasonable profits.

3. Guarantee of equality between Indians and non-Indians.

4. Equal representation by patriotic, popular, and democratic sectors in the new government, equal rights for women, protection for children, and guarantees of freedom of expression and religion.

5. National self-determination and a policy of nonalignment and international cooperation.

The sketchy nature of the URNG's political platform has made the URNG an unknown quantity in many respects. Its failure to present a more detailed platform for political and economic change may also explain its failure to develop an infrastructure of support among the popular sectors, the popular movement, and those Guatemalans of progressive political tendencies. As it entered into the peace talks in 1990, the URNG's exact political and economic demands still remained unclear.

The Military Front

The military high command in the late 1980s toasted victory in the counterinsurgency war. All that remained of the guerrilla armies were small isolated bands that constituted no real military threat. Defense Minister Gramajo went so far as to say that conflictive zones no longer existed. But those who traveled through the country's rugged interior painted a different reality.

Throughout many areas of the northern highlands and the FTN, army patrols acknowledged that the hills still belonged to the guerrillas. While the army was militarily stronger, it had failed to instill "security" in the conflictive zones. Road-building plans were stymied by guerrilla sabotage, and guerrilla units still seized villages for propaganda sessions. Stepped-up use of civil patrols for scouting missions and large-scale military offensives also testified to the continued guerrilla threat. This reality of enduring guerrilla war was highlighted by the protests of the army's own Officers of the Mountain, who charged that the desk generals were living the good life while they were underequipped and unable to count on the full support of the government.

Military and political initiatives by URNG have proved the continued viability of the guerrilla movement. The URNG has not pretended to wield a military force capable of directly confronting the Guatemalan army with major offensive operations. Instead of frontal assaults, it has waged an escalating war of attrition relying mainly on ambushes, sabotage, and attacks on isolated military outposts.

Despite military claims that the guerrillas arc simply isolated bands of terrorists, the URNG has demonstrated its ability to mount geographically diverse and well-coordinated military operations. In 1988 it launched its first joint offensives involving all four guerrilla armies, and the number of its operations doubled in 1989. By 1990 the URNG had forces active in 12 departments and the country's two largest cities.[10]

It was regularly mounting operations along the south coast and in the central highlands. The URNG claims that it is slowly accumulating forces so that at the proper political opportunity it will be able to launch a major offensive. Boasts by the military that it defeated the guerrillas have repeatedly proved false. Stalled army offensives in the highlands and lightning guerrilla attacks in Guatemala City and Quezaltenango in the late 1980s testified to mounting URNG strength. Government estimates put the number of guerrillas at under 1,000 while other more objective sources that there are 1,500 to 2,000 guerrillas.[11] News sources close to the URNG have reported a guerrilla force of 3,500. To increase its military potential, the URNG has developed a crude weapons industry, including the manufacture of mines and artillery.

Although the URNG has shown itself to be more than a band of leftist terrorists, as the military has repeatedly claimed, it has still failed to regain a substantial infrastructure of active popular support. It has proved capable of mounting operations throughout much of the country but it is still the Guatemalan army that controls the rural population. In an apparent effort to develop more popular support, the URNG has begun to mount more nonmilitary operations in which guerrilla troops occupy villages and explain their political position to gathered villagers.

To constitute itself as a political force to be reckoned with the URNG, in addition to winning broad popular support, also has to demonstrate that has the military capability to challenge the Guatemalan army. With the stepped-up levels of sabotage and attacks on military targets in the late 1980s, the URNG did indeed win increased recognition as a military force but its operations still fell more in the category of harassment than actual military conflict.

Talking About Peace

Speaking for URNG, Pablo Monsanto, the commander of FAR, stated that the guerrilla armies are fighting for "a neutral, independent country able to decide for itself its destiny and not one subjected to the interests of other nations." The primary goal is to negotiate a solution to the conflict, he emphasized. The military tactic of wearing down the army is viewed as essential to the political goal of forcing the army and government to the negotiating table. According to Monsanto:

> We believe that the crisis can be solved if all the political, social, progressive, nationalist, revolutionary, democratic, and humanitarian groups come to an agreement and draft a new project for the development of the country, in which the military limits itself to the defense of the national territory....Their only mission is defense.[12]

Since 1985 the URNG has called for negotiations to resolve the conflict. It has also demanded the right to participate in the national dialogue that was created as a result of the Esquipulas II peace accords. With the exception of a brief meeting in October 1987, all the URNG's offers were ignored or dismissed by the government until April 1990. Diplomatic and military initiatives by the URNG and international pressure then resulted in the government's agreeing to open a dialogue with the guerrilla command. (See Peace Process)

The initiation of the peace talks raised questions about the political direction and unity of the URNG. Is it really the hope of the URNG command to present itself as a contending political force in the electoral arena or did it believe that only by mounting a strong revolutionary war could the control of the army and the oligarchy be successfully contested? In fact, it would seem likely that if the URNG did attempt to operate openly in the political process its leaders and cadres would be quickly eliminated by the security forces and associated death squads. In the late 1960s, something similar occurred when the guerrilla army threw its support behind the candidacy of Mario Méndez Montenegro. Soon after assuming the presidency, Méndez Montenegro appointed General Carlos Arana as Minister of Defense. Arana then unleashed an unprecedented campaign of terror against the guerrillas and suspected supporters.

In all likelihood the guerrilla insurgency and the counterinsurgency war will continue. For the government and the military, counterinsurgency has become, after more than 25 years of fighting, a type of governance and a way of life. The profound misery of the population and country's deep class and race divisions, combined with the repressive ways of the security forces and the failure of democratic institutions to address social tensions, incite political violence.

Chapter 3

Economy

The State of the Economy

During the 1960s and until the late 1970s the Guatemalan economy was boosted by 5 percent or more annual growth rates. But a slump in the world market combined with escalating internal political turmoil resulted in a sharp economic downturn that burdened the country with negative growth rates until 1987. Bolstered by a sudden influx of multilateral and bilateral aid, the Cerezo government managed to pull the economy out of its recession. Even so, the growth rates of the late 1980s barely kept up with yearly population increases.

Having ruled out the feasibility of strong reform measures, the Cerezo government chose to address widening social inequity with handout programs financed by foreign private and government agencies. It backed away from demands for substantial increases in the minimum wage, price controls on basic goods, agrarian reform, assistance to small farmers, and protection for workers' rights. Although it did push through — with the support of the army — somewhat higher income and production taxes, most attempts to institute measures that would adversely affect the private-sector elite were only half-heartedly pursued or quickly dropped. All things considered, the Christian Democratic government proved to be more concerned with short-term economic growth statistics than the broader public welfare. Although the economy had achieved a modicum of stability by 1990, there was little hope that socioeconomic conditions would improve under the selected model of growth that stressed private-sector investment and export production.

The most striking trait of the Guatemalan economy during the late 1980s was its recovery from a period of negative growth in the first half of the 1980s. From 1986 to 1989 the economy grew at an annual rate of 2.5 to 4 percent. This rate of growth did not, however, begin to recover the levels of national income achieved before the economic crisis set in during the late 1970s. Nonetheless, the Christian Democratic government pointed to several years of positive economic growth as evidence of its successful policies.

Other indicators also supported the Christian Democratic contention that the economy was on the right track. Between 1986 and 1989 the public-sector deficit steadily declined, export income increased, tax revenues were up, and inflation was kept at manageable levels. Outside the party, however, few Guatemalans were content with the country's economic performance.

The most vocal and powerful critics are found in the private sector, represented mainly by a business organization, Coordinating Committee of Agricultural, Commercial, Industrial, and Financial Associations (CACIF). Its critique of the government's economic policies focuses on several issues: a corrupt and bloated public sector budget, insufficient government support for private-sector investment, too many government-imposed financial constraints (taxes and duties) on business activity, and the failure of the government to consult the private sector on key decisions.

Also strongly opposing the government's economic policies were unions and activist organizations that compose the popular movement, as represented by the UASP coalition. In marked contrast to CACIF, UASP claimed that government economic policies almost exclusively benefited the business elite, especially the agroexport sector. It complained that the government's stabilization policy victimized poor and working people while benefiting the wealthy.

During the late 1980s the country experienced some new investment in nontraditional agricultural and industrial production, but overall the value of the country's exports was no greater than in 1980.[1] Conditions for the country's poor majority deteriorated in the 1980s as the prices of basic goods rose dramatically, unemployment and underemployment affected over half of the workforce, and wages remained at unlivable levels. At the end of the decade per capita income in Guatemala was no greater than it was in 1970. Some 87 percent of the population was living in poverty — up from 79 percent in 1980 — and at least half the country's families could not even afford a minimally adequate diet let alone other necessities.[2]

Wealth is becoming ever more concentrated. Between 1970 and 1984, the percentage of national income captured by the top 20 percent increased from 45.5 percent to 56.8 percent. The minimum wage — about $1.16 a day in early 1990 — provides less than a worker needs to cover basic needs. In the 1980s, all the social indicators of adequate housing, health, education, and nutrition declined.

Economic Picture Darkens

By 1990 the macroeconomic recovery began to disintegrate in the facing of rising public deficits, severe widening of the commercial trade deficit, alarming inflation, and sharp reductions in international aid. In early 1990 the government let the national currency bloat, causing a dramatic devaluation of the *quetzal*. The devaluation, while gratifying Washington, international banks, and the export elite, caused an immediate deterioration in the standard of living as prices for basic goods doubled and tripled. At the end of its term, the Christian Democratic government was also feeling the economic crunch. It could no longer meet its budget commitments to the municipalities and numerous ministries found themselves without funds to carry out essential government services.

In devaluating the currency, the government acceded to the demands of the agroexport sector and international lenders. It also moved to implement other elements of the neoliberal agenda, such as removing customs barriers on imports, raising rates for government services, and taking the price lid off basic services and transportation. It was the hope that these measures would not only satisfy private-sector critics but would also open the doors to new loans from the World Bank and the International Monetary Fund (IMF) — both of which had declared Guatemala out of compliance with previously agreed upon structural-adjustment programs. Guatemala was also in arrears with the Inter-American Development Bank (IDB).

The economic prospects for the 1990s are less than hopeful despite the small measure of growth and stability achieved in the late 1980s. Among the major characteristics and weaknesses of the economy as it entered the new decade were the following:

* Reliance on large injections of bilateral and multilateral foreign aid that are now steadily declining.

* A widening trade imbalance owing to increased imports and a disappointing export trade.

* Deterioration of domestic and regional markets owing in large part to austerity measures and an almost exclusive emphasis on extra-regional exports.

* A $2.7 billion (1989) external debt — equivalent to 60 percent of the gross national product and 42 percent of export earnings — which

has led to a worsening debt-service crunch as interest rates rise and short-term debt comes due.

* Continued heavy dependence on agroexports (about 75 percent of total exports) in a time of depressed world prices for its main exports, especially coffee.

* Despite government efforts, the country's tax burden is one of the lightest in the world, which obstructs desperately needed increases in funding for government social services while forcing the government to rely on bilateral and multilateral aid for virtually all public-sector infrastructure projects. It has been estimated that the private sector avoids paying at least 40 percent of the taxes it owes the government, forcing the public sector to depend on regressive indirect taxes, like the sales tax, and injections of foreign aid to cover over 80 percent of budgetary expenses.

* A reactionary private sector dominated by agroexport-based oligarchs obstructs the kind of reforms (agrarian reform, expanded organizing rights, higher minimum wages, and increased direct taxes on income and property) that would contribute to a modernization of the economy and a broadening of the internal market.

* Dependence on public-sector spending to bolster the economy while private sector investment remains low.

* Continuing pressure to increase the pace of currency devaluation.

* Dramatic worsening of conditions for the poor majority in the face of unprecedented inflation.

A flood of foreign aid and a mixture of fiscal and monetary reforms pulled the Guatemalan economy out of its period of stagnation in the early 1980s. But the economic improvements of the late 1980s showed no sign of resolving the main challenges of the Guatemalan economy: 1) improving the welfare of the poor majority and thereby easing the socioeconomic roots of popular rebellion, and 2) establishing a base for steady economic growth. Instead, socioeconomic conditions are worsening, and the much-touted economic stability of the "new Guatemala" seem more like a house of cards that could sway and topple with small changes in the international economic and political winds.

Modern Oligarchs

In Guatemala, the private sector maintains an elevated view of itself and its place in society. Not just part of a wider society, the elite private sector lords over the nation like a feudal oligarch. For the business community, anything that contravenes its short-term interests smacks of socialism. Its most extreme members (by no means the minority) even criticized the Cerezo government for its socialist tendencies.

Dominated by the coffee growers, this agroexport oligarchy and associated mercantile interests exercised undisputed control over the society until 1944 when a democratic alliance overthrew General Jorge Ubico. For ten years, the most progressive sectors of the economic elite attempted to reform and modernize Guatemala. Although the traditional oligarchy, together with the most reactionary political elements in the country, succeeded in crushing this experiment in capitalist modernization, many of its economic reforms persisted—such as the creation of a broader economic infrastructure and the encouragement given to new business associations.

Over the last 35 years the traditional agroexport oligarchy with its inveterate conservatism has remained powerful, although new commercial, financial, and industrial interests have been integrated into oligarchic circles. Although it now counts on a broader economic base, the private sector maintains its narrow-minded and self-interested character as well as an unrelenting opposition to economic reforms that might threaten its immediate interests.

The most dramatic change in the country's power structure in the last several decades has been its reduced power relative to the armed forces. Four factors—the military's own economic investments, its increased professionalism, the expanded militarization of the country, and the army's broader political/economic vision—account for this challenge to traditional oligarchic dominance.

Inside the Oligarchy

The Guatemalan oligarchy is a netherworld where questions of politics and economics blend together and where differences are often solved by force rather than by negotiation. The oligarchy does not stand behind one political party. Rather it tends to think of itself as a political power in its own right, negotiating directly with the government and military rather than lobbying for its interests through a political party.

The oligarchy remains a force that neither the army nor the government can afford to ignore. Its power is concentrated in CACIF. If the government wants to alter economic policy, it has to contend with the opinions and economic might of CACIF. Founded in 1957, CACIF represents the collective interests of the traditional private sector. It serves as the supreme council of all the different business sectors, each of which have their own chamber. UNAGRO, for example, is the chamber that represents the agribusiness sector.

Although it sometimes may appear so, the Guatemalan private sector does not speak with one voice. Each of the chambers has its own perspective, some more conservative than others. While there are differences within CACIF, its enduring function is to protect the interests and the standing of the country's wealthiest families. In chorus with CACIF, three other private-sector associations also promote and defend the interests of the business elite: Association of Friends of the Country, Chamber of Entrepreneurs, and Chamber of Free Enterprise.

The Association of the Friends of the Country (Amigos del País), founded in 1795, has historically represented the most traditional and conservative elements of the oligarchy. In the late 1980s, however, it was receiving funds from the Agency for International Development (AID) and had become part of modernizing trend within the oligarchy, which, while adamantly rejecting the least hint of structural reform, has accepted the need for more stable political institutions. Friends of the Country publishes books and popular-education materials designed to strengthen the private sector. Of a common stripe is the Chamber of Entrepreneurs (CAEM), an association of businessmen founded with AID funds in 1981 as part of its Private Sector Strengthening project. Originally created to challenge the predominance of CACIF, CAEM has become more like a developmental organization specializing in the promotion of investment in nontraditional exports. A third group, the Chamber of Free Enterprise, serves as a forum for an ideology of uncompromising neoliberalism of the type taught at the Francisco Marroquín University.

An influential sector of modernizers, which has pushed for a concerted government-business commitment to nontraditional agricultural and industrial export production, emerged among the private sector elite in the 1980s. These modernizers, operating through the new business associations funded by AID, have also promoted a new rhetoric that equates economic and political freedoms.

Spurred on by a flurry of AID private-sector strengthening projects, the business elite has become more sophisticated in its self-promotion. This new finesse has taken the form of cloaking reactionary demands in the rhetoric of democratization. To defend its immediate interests, the private sector has also attempted to popularize neoliberalism, using slogans like "What is good for Business is good for the Country" and "I too am a businessman." In its opposition to tax hikes in 1987, CACIF paid for an advertisement that screamed, "Big Government, Poor People." For its part, the Chamber of Industry warned Guatemalans: "Private property does not only refer to big capital. Your plot, your house, your car, everything you own are also private property."[3]

In the past, during the long decades of overt military rule, the oligarchy never saw itself as a champion of democracy. But adapting to the new spirit of "democratization," the oligarchy has seized the rhetoric of democracy as its own. It now argues that there exists a one-to-one correspondence between democracy and economic freedom. When opposing a government or army initiative, business organizations invariably haul out the constitution or "Magna Carta" as some like to call it, charging that the sacred constitutional and democratic rights of all Guatemalans are being trampled upon.

In the name of democracy, the modern oligarchs attack taxes and increased minimum wages as infringements on their economic freedom. The sanctity of democratic freedoms has also been called upon in the oligarchy's opposition to the government/military policy of "active neutrality" and in its refusal to dialogue with the popular movement.

While a neoliberal economic philosophy accents the rhetoric of the today's oligarchy, the private sector is, as a whole, more pragmatic than ideological. Except for a small faction of intellectuals, neoliberalism is more an instrument of attack than a set of operating principles. It adopts the rhetoric of neoliberalism only when its suits its interests — as in its opposition to government price controls. Rather than calling for the complete liberalization of the economy and elimination of all government intervention, the oligarchy demands that the state function as its servant. As CACIF is well aware, many elements within the private sector depend on government intervention and investment. Sugar producers, for example, profit from high domestic price levels set by the government. Domestic industry still relies on government protections, and the construction industry is propped up by public-sector investment. Even the export sector, while espousing neoliberalism, often pressures the government to expand public-sector services (infrastructure, irrigation projects, marketing and credit assistance) available to exporters.

When its immediate interests are threatened, the private sector in Guatemala is not accustomed to compromise. It accepted the government's policy of *concertación* only when the government adopted private-sector recommendations — while rejecting all measures designed to meet the demands of the poor majority. While trying to maintain some semblance of policy independence, the Cerezo government consistently bowed to the demands of CACIF. But it has never bowed low enough for CACIF's liking. All the ills of the economy are laid at the feet of the government.

Both the government and CACIF agree that private-sector investment needs to be the motor of national economic growth. But that investment has not been forthcoming, despite a cascade of government incentives including reduction of export taxes and liberalization of prices. Traditionally, the private sector in Guatemala declines to invest its own money in productive ventures, preferring instead to rely on government and foreign credit.

What little investment the private sector has demonstrated has been in areas where its way has been paved with subsidies and incentives provided by the government and AID. Only in construction – the traditional piggybank of the rich – has the private sector shown any real inclination to invest. Instead of sinking capital into the future of Guatemala, the private sector, thus far, has tended to blame the government for the failure to provide a secure investment climate. With starvation wages, a terrorized labor sector, and an array of new incentives to promote private-sector investment, one might ask what more would CACIF need to be satisfied.

Throughout the 1980s the oligarchy of Guatemala maintained its essentially reactionary character – refusing to countenance economic policies that would more evenly distribute the country's wealth and resorting to coup-mongering when its interests were threatened. In terms of widening the economic base of capitalism in Guatemala, there has been more reformist thinking among the military than among the country's oligarchy. Back in the early 1970s, General Arana, frustrated with the country's hidebound private sector, announced his intention to "modernize capitalism in Guatemala, no matter what the cost." This reformism played a part in the army's support for the National Reconstruction Committee. More recently, it could be seen in its support for limited democratization and its call for the private sector to help pay the "social debt" and contribute more to the maintenance of the state.

Talk by the Cerezo government and the military of paying the "social debt" was dismissed by virtually all sectors of the oligarchy as "uneconomic" thinking. Bolstered by the tenets of neoliberal philosophy and the private-sector development philosophy proffered by AID, modern oligarchs say, instead, that the type of reformism needed in Guatemala is of an economic not social character – namely reforms designed to strengthen their immediate financial prospects within the traditional context of an export economy. In this demand for economic reforms (reduced export taxes, investment incentives, privatization, liberalized prices, etc.), there is a coincidence of interests among most private-sector factions.

There does exist a small, silent minority of businessmen which sees its interests tied to an expansion of the domestic market. These entrepreneurs, who feel stifled both by the lack of a large domestic base of consumers and the monopoly control of the private-sector elite (as represented by CACIF), would support the kind of economic and social reforms needed to modernize the Guatemalan economy. But to articulate such social democratic sentiments is regarded as treasonous among the private sector and, in some cases, has spelled death sentences for these would-be reformers.

Agriculture

The economic crisis has drawn Guatemalans to the city at a rapid rate. Nonetheless, the country's economic mainstay continues to be the agricultural sector—which accounts for about 25 percent of national income, employs 58 percent of the active workforce, and provides about 75 percent of the country's foreign exchange. In Latin America, only in Haiti and Honduras does such a high percentage of the population work in the agricultural sector.

Perhaps more clearly than in any other Central American country, Guatemala has two agricultural economies. The dominant economy is one of commercial estates located mostly along the fertile south coast and secondarily to the north in the department of Izabal. The extreme concentration of land and an export orientation characterizes this dominant agricultural economy. Paralleling the agroexport economy is a system of peasant agriculture, characterized by small plots of land devoted to subsistence agriculture. These two economies—while markedly different—are interdependent. The peasant economy of *minifundios* (small parcels) serves to keep wage rates low in Guatemala by enabling a large sector of the peasant population to survive and feed themselves during the off-seasons, facilitating temporary work during the harvest seasons for substandard wages paid by the agroexport estates.[4]

Land Reform

No other issue in Guatemala is so volatile as the use and ownership of land. It is an issue that sparked a CIA-sponsored coup in 1954 and later gave rise to death squads and civil war. As Guatemala enters the 1990s, the inequities resulting from skewed patterns of land ownership and use continue to divide its society and stifle its economic development.

In 1952 the Arbenz government instituted an agrarian reform as part of its plan to rid the country of its feudal elements and open the doors to a more modern capitalist economy. For the landed oligarchs, the Catholic church, and United Fruit Company, agrarian reform meant godless communism — in other words, the loss of land and privilege. That attempt at economic modernization was aborted by the 1954 coup, and the country has suffered the political and economic consequences ever since.

Despite harsh repression, the issue of land reform will not go away. Fewer than 2 percent of the landowners own 65 percent of the farmland — the most highly skewed land-tenure pattern in Latin America. This land-tenure situation is compounded by the fact that most postage-stamp plots of land straddle mountain slopes while the richest land is held by the largest producers. According to AID, about a third of the population lives on farms too small or too poor to support a family.[5]

One result of this skewed land distribution is that 80 percent of rural Guatemalans live in absolute poverty, unable even to satisfy their most basic needs. Another result is that the country can no longer feed itself since the best land and all technical assistance serves agroexport production by mostly large landowners. Such conditions explain the widespread support among Guatemalan peasants for the guerrilla forces in the early 1980s.

In 1986 Padre Andrés Girón and his Pro-Land Peasant Association dared to put agrarian reform once again on the national agenda. A year before, presidential candidate Vinicio Cerezo had promised the Union of Agricultural Producers (UNAGRO) that his government would not institute an agrarian reform. He said he would not even mention land reform because "to use the term in this country causes emotional reactions." Shortly after Cerezo's inauguration, Girón led 16,000 campesinos, mainly from the south coast, to the National Palace to demand that the government distribute land to the landless.

Even though Girón's movement was not demanding that the government expropriate land, only that it redistribute land purchased from private owners, the Pro-Land organization stirred vitriolic opposition from UNAGRO and large landowners. The Pro-Land leaders argued, in the Social Christian tradition, that their movement represented an alternative to communism and arbitrary land expropriations. But the hardliners of UNAGRO felt any government involvement in land redistribution, even in controlled land sales, would open the way to wholesale agrarian reform.

The government did eventually respond favorably to the Pro-Land movement. Several estates were sold to the Girón organization, but this token measure fell far short of the great need for land and could scarcely be termed an agrarian reform. Instead it represented an extension of a land-sales program financed by AID and implemented by the Penny Foundation with the approval of UNAGRO. As an added onus, the Girón movement, rather than paying back the foundation, had to pay the government for land sold to them at higher than market-value prices.

Agrarian reform again came to the fore when the Catholic bishops in 1988 circulated a pastoral letter called "The Cry for Land." While the bishops offered no concrete remedies, they did conclude that "it is necessary and urgent to change our country's sinful and obsolete social structures." Acting quickly to distance itself from the Catholic church, the Cerezo government pledged, "There will be no agrarian reform." For its part, UNAGRO reproved the bishops asserting that it "rejects any project or idea that looks or smells like expropriatory agrarian reform." Even AID has concluded that the country needs agrarian reform, although recognizing that political conditions within Guatemala make it unfeasible.

Traditional Exports

Coffee, which accounts for about 40 percent of the country's income, is grown virtually everywhere in Guatemala, except for the departments of Petén and Totonicapán. While some 60,000 farms produce coffee, more than 75 percent of the coffee comes from fewer than 5 percent of the country's coffee estates.

Coffee production gave rise to the Guatemalan oligarchy. Many of the country's wealthiest families—including Aragón Quiñones, Plocharsky, Brol, and Falla—own vast coffee estates. According to the U.S. Department of Agriculture, the coffee estates in Guatemala are among the largest in the world. Unlike in many other coffee-producing nations, export trade is not nationalized in Guatemala. As a consequence, a great deal of the income from the coffee business flows into the coffers of the export houses. These private companies not only arrange the sale of Guatemalan coffee on the international market but also finance coffee production itself.[6] The United States buys slightly over half of the country's coffee exports. The termination of international quotas and the resulting drop in coffee prices in 1989 cast a dark shadow over the coffee industry. Producers responded by pressuring the government to devalue the currency in 1990, leading to windfall profits.

Bananas bring in about 8 percent of the country's foreign-currency income. As a function of rising international prices, banana income rose steadily in the late 1980s. All banana production is located in the departments of Izabal and Zacapa—the low-lying northern area that faces the Caribbean. Del Monte (subsidiary of R.J. Reynolds) dominates the banana export business and controls 80 percent of production through its local branch BANDEGUA. Six independent producers (organized as the Independent Banana Company or COBIGUA) account for the other 20 percent. During the 1980s, *solidarista* associations began to replace labor unions in the banana industry. (See Labor and Unions) Seventy percent of Guatemalan bananas enter the U.S. market.[7]

The two other major agroexports—sugar and cotton—experienced hard times in the 1980s, although they are now recovering due to increased international prices and demand. Most of the country's sugar comes from Escuintla on the south coast, where extensive sugar estates and giant mills dominate the land. The local sugar industry was sustained during years of low prices by a strong domestic demand and fixed prices on the local market. Pressure from the sugar oligarchs resulted in a doubling in guaranteed sugar prices in the mid-1980s. One of those benefiting from artificially high domestic prices was the Botrán family, which in addition to owning a sugar mill produces the country's brand of rum. The United States, under its sugar quota system, buys about 40 percent of Guatemala's sugar exports.

Cotton production suffered a major decline in the 1980s, dropping to a 25-year low in 1987. Although cotton production has since recovered somewhat, the industry is but a thin shadow of its former self. Like sugar, cotton production is concentrated on the south coast. The cotton industry is extremely concentrated in Guatemala—just 15 families control half the production. The average size of a Guatemalan cotton estate was 638 hectares in 1979, compared to 25 to 40 hectares for the rest of Central America.[8]

As elsewhere in the region, the expansion of the beef industry over the past 25 years has been devastating for both Indian communities and the environment. Whereas the agroexport boom in cotton and sugar did not extend beyond the south coast, the rise of the beef industry has affected some of the most isolated and previously unspoiled areas of the country. Using peasant colonists to clear the land, the beef industry has leveled great expanses of tropical forests the last four decades. It was just this type of expansion that led to the Panzós massacre of some one hundred Kekchí Indians in 1978, after cattle growers complained to the military that the Indians were protesting their land-grabbing. All beef exports—which constitute over one-fifth of local production—are shipped to the United States.[9]

Nontraditional Exports

The promotion of nontraditional agroexports is nothing new in Guatemala. In the 1950s and 1960s, international lending institutions promoted the cotton, beef, and sugar industries as a way to diversify the economy's dependence on coffee and bananas. In the 1970s, AID undertook a new type of agricultural diversification, this time promoting vegetables, flowers, and spices. These nontraditionals, which developed gradually in the 1980s, account for about 10 percent of total agroexports – about the same level they represented ten years ago. Although there have been increases in some nontraditional exports in the late 1980s, declining sales in other products and continuing problems with regional market have kept nontraditionals from advancing beyond former export levels.

Nontraditionals face many of the same problems of more established agroexports like coffee and cotton including oscillating prices and shrinking markets. The oscillations of the world market are compounded for nontraditional agroexport producers because the markets for which they produce are generally smaller. There is also more risk involved since nontraditional exports usually spoil faster and crops commonly require more frequent applications of fertilizer and pesticides, augmenting a farmer's risk.

The rise and fall of cardamom production in Guatemala amply illustrates the underlying problems of diversification into nontraditionals. In the mid-1970s, Guatemala entered the cardamom market and by 1986 was supplying over 60 percent of world demand. In the development pole of Playa Grande, AID and CARE used food-for-work and agricultural-development programs to integrate peasants into this cardamom boom. Cardamom had become one of the country's leading sources of foreign exchange, and accounted for nearly half of nontraditional agroexports.[10]

By 1988 the world's small market for cardamom (mainly the Arab countries) had become saturated. Other countries – Costa Rica, Ecuador, Honduras, and India – had joined Guatemala in the cardamom exporting business, and prices plummeted. So weak was the market that nearly half of the country's cardamom exporters did no business in 1988, and peasant farmers who had been growing cardamom in the Northern Transverse Strip were left without any source of income and with a harvest they could not eat.

There is little doubt that the agricultural sector needs to pursue diversification, but it is a development path fraught with difficulties. While the diversification into fruit and vegetable production was boosted by the Caribbean Basin Initiative (CBI), Guatemalan producers have discovered that the U.S. market is a fickle creature. Competition from nontraditional agroexport sectors in other Caribbean Basin countries, mainly the Dominican Republic and Costa Rica, also narrows the market space for Guatemalan products. Protectionism by U.S. producers and new consumer concerns about pesticide-saturated produce cast a further shadow over the future of diversification attempts.

Although nontraditional agroexports often spell high profit margins, they also involve high costs of production. It costs a producer of snow peas about $4,000 a hectare in contrast to only $250 to $375 a hectare (ranging from manual to mechanized production) for corn or $750 to produce a technified hectare of coffee.[11] While AID poses nontraditional agroexport production as an alternative for Guatemalan farmers, it is generally a gamble only affordable to commercial-level farmers, not the hundreds of thousands of peasant farmers that cultivate the country's poorest land.

Food Production

Since 1980, basic grains production (corn, beans, and rice) has failed to keep pace with population growth. While production of traditional and nontraditional exports increased at a brisk pace, basic grains increased at the rate of one percent a year — far below the 3 percent rate of population growth. As a result, the country has had to import an increasing proportion of its basic grains. Neither can Guatemala meet its need for dairy products. The country has the lowest rate of milk production in Latin America — providing an average daily per capita allotment of only two tablespoons.

The U.S. Department of Agriculture (USDA) estimates that to achieve self-sufficiency, corn acreage would have to increase from 690,000 to 775,000 hectares. Yet, due in part to U.S. development policies, acreage previously devoted to basic grains is being converted to export crops.[12]

Farmers have little incentive to grow basic grains despite this shortfall in production. Food imports from the United States undercut the local market and keep prices low. Since 1984, Guatemala has received an increasing amount of U.S. food aid. According to USDA, "Nearly all of Guatemala's agricultural commodity imports come from the United States, and since 1985, virtually all U.S. origin imports have been donated or financed under concessional and commercial assistance programs."[13]

The Guatemalan government does have a policy of food security with the stated objective of promoting local food production, but it has not been enforced. In fact, the government has welcomed increasing food aid to ease budget deficits and to pacify targeted social sectors (urban slums and displaced families in conflictive areas) with food aid. Both the army and the government share the concern that food shortages and high food prices will increase social tensions. But rather than initiate the kind of sectoral adjustment needed to prioritize food security, food aid and cheap food imports have provided a short-term avoidance mechanism.

Industry and Tourism

The industrial sector boomed in the 1960s and 1970s as a result of the Central America Common Market (CACM). As the Central America market began to constrict in the late 1970s, so did the Guatemalan industrial sector. Today, the manufacturing companies of Guatemala long for the days of an expanding CACM while searching for new customers overseas. The industrial sector, which developed behind high tariff barriers, recognizes the need to diversify its outlets while fighting to retain its historic economic privileges. In this sense, domestic industry feels threatened by the advances of neoliberalism and the pressure of the World Bank and the IMF to tear down protectionist tariffs.

Although the most developed manufacturing sector in Central America, industry accounts for only 16 percent of Guatemala's national income. The bulk of manufacturing is found in the food processing and beverage industries, while pharmaceuticals manufactured by foreign companies lead the list of industrial exports. The industrial sector has traditionally been based in the CACM. Even today, the country's industrial sector (which is dominated by foreign corporations) accounts for 45 percent of intra-regional export trade.

Less than one hundred manufacturing firms employ 100 or more workers in Guatemala, and now most of these firms operate at much less than full capacity. With AID's encouragement and financing, there is a new emphasis on assembly-export manufacturing (drawback industry). Today, there are 225 assembly plants employing some 50,000 workers who piece together clothing and sew in the labels of dozens of U.S. lines, including Levi-Strauss, Van Heusen, Calvin Klein, Liz Claiborne, and Arrow. Most of the plants are owned locally although there is also substantial South Korean investment in these plants that aim to take advantage of the CBI trade incentives.[14]

But many local investors are skeptical. One Guatemalan industrialist found that after two years of exporting textiles to the United States he was being squeezed out of the market by investors in the Dominican Republic. Confidence in the textile sector was also deflated by a 1989 reduction in the U.S. import quota.

In the 1970s, Guatemala hoped to expand industry through mining and oil ventures, but these diversification dreams have been dissolved. Large nickel mining operations near Lake Izabal were shut down in 1981. Guatemala does produce oil, but foreign sales by the end of the decade had dropped 70 percent from a record high in 1983. In a setback to the country's plan to reduce its dependence on the agricultural sector, Amoco Corporation announced in early 1989 that it was discontinuing its oil exploration project in the Franja Transversal — complaining that it suffered a constant siege by guerrillas. Like Amoco, other foreign companies have suspended exploration operations, and production by Basic Resources, another private oil corporation, has not met the high expectations of the company and the government.

Although not as contentious an issue as in other Central American countries, privatization of public-sector corporations is underway in Guatemala. The first company targeted is Aviateca airline, which the military has hamstrung through abuse for the personal benefit of its officers. CACIF is also pressuring the government to privatize the telephone company (GUATEL), the national railroad system (FEGUA), and the electricity company (INDE).

One of the most hopeful signs for the economy during the 1980s was the steady growth of the tourism industry. Recovering from the slump of the early 1980s, largely attributable to the then-raging counterinsurgency war, the industry was booming by 1986. In 1989, tourism ranked third after coffee and nontraditional exports as a source of foreign exchange. The country's improved international image as the result of the slowdown in counterinsurgency operations and the transition to civilian rule accounted for the new influx of tourists. The industry also benefited from increased international publicity about the tropical rainforests and Mayan ruins in the country. Foreign investors, like Club Med (which is considering establishing an "archaeological villa" near Tikal), have expressed increasing interest in profiting from this upswing in tourism. By 1990, however, increasing human rights violations and guerrilla advances, as well as an expanded State Department travel advisory, began to dampen prospects for continued growth in this important economic sector.

Chapter 4

Society and Environment

Popular Organizing

The 1954 coup and subsequent repression of the organized popular movement cast Guatemala into a kind of political winter. It was not until the early 1970s that the popular movement began to recuperate. The teachers' strike of 1973 and the formation of the National Committee of Trade Union Unity (CNUS) in 1976 marked a renewal in urban organizing, while the courageous march of the Huehuetenango miners in 1977 and the founding of the Campesino Unity Committee (CUC) in 1978 signaled the rise of the rural popular movement. In early 1979 a popular coalition called the Democratic Front Against Repression (FDCR) formed, bringing together virtually every active progressive and democratic organization.

As the popular movement grew, repression escalated. The January 31, 1980 burning of the Spanish embassy occupied by 39 protesters including 27 CUC members and supporters measured the horrible lengths the military government would go to repress popular organizing. Still, popular organizations continued to struggle and in 1981 some came together to form the January 31 Popular Front (FP-31), which offered itself as a "unitary structure to deepen support and coordination between mass organizations." This popular alliance, however, was short-lived due to the mounting wave of terror spread by the Lucas García regime.

As the counterinsurgency war began losing intensity in 1983, room for popular organizing gradually increased. An early sign of this opportunity was the formation in 1983 of the CUSG labor confederation promoted by the Ríos Montt government. Gradually, as the military proceeded with its institutional reform project, other popular groups began to establish themselves, the first of which was the Mutual Support Group (GAM), founded in 1985. The creation of the UNSITRAGUA labor confederation in 1985 was another attempt to test the political opening. In the second half of the decade the popular movement also took on broader dimensions with the formation of women's groups and human rights organizations, complemented by a surge in organizing by the displaced population and Indian farmworkers.

The Clamor for Land

It was the issue of inequitable land distribution, however, that spurred the first mass organizing since the late 1970s. The spark that ignited this peasant organizing was a maverick Catholic priest, Andrés Girón, a rotund padre with a flair for publicity. Girón tapped the deep-felt need of the south coast peasants for agrarian reform. From his parish in Nueva Concepción, Padre Girón organized the Pro-Land Peasant Association to demand land from the new Christian Democratic government. This movement of over 100,000 peasants dared to call for agrarian reform and took their demands directly to the National Palace in several impressive mass demonstrations.

Girón's movement gradually lost steam but it did pave the way for the reemergence of other peasant groups, notably CUC. Unlike the Pro-Land movement, CUC was not demanding that the government sell land to landless campesinos. It focused, instead, on the plight of the farmworker. Before being driven underground in 1981, CUC organized a highly effective strike against the sugar mills of the south coast. In early 1989, as it surfaced from hiding, it organized numerous strikes against the large estates and mills of the southern coastal plains. As many as 50,000 laborers also joined a brief and unsuccessful CUC strike organized in early 1990.

The Popular Alliance

In late 1987 the popular movement and the labor movement collaborated to form the Labor and Popular Action Unity (UASP) alliance to present a united front in the face of repression and government unresponsiveness. The leading member of this new popular coalition was the UNSITRAGUA labor confederation, but it was based on the collective strength of the entire popular movement. Members of UASP included two human rights groups (GAM and CONAVIGUA), two student organizations (AEU and the secondary students' organization, CEEM), numerous unions (UNSITRAGUA, FESEBS, STINDE, STEG, FENASTEG, and Luz y Fuerza), a progressive religious association called the Monsignor Romero Group, CUC, South Coast Workers Alliance, the Council of the Displaced (CONDEG), and two Indian rights groups (the Highland Campesino Committee and the Runajel Junam Council of Ethnic Communities, known as CERJ).

In 1988 UASP presented a list of demands to the National Reconciliation Commission (See Peace Process) that constituted a platform for moderate social change in Guatemala. This call for change incorporated the full spectrum of demands of the popular movement, ranging from respect for human rights to a moratorium on external debt payments and an end to sexual harassment and discrimination.

Other than its role in joining important elements of the popular sector in a single coalition, UASP could point to few concrete achievements. Its major success—the March 1988 negotiation with the government for a price freeze on basic goods and wage increases—was reversed by a May 1988 coup attempt by dissident officers. Searching for a way out of his dilemma, Cerezo ignored the agreements he made with UASP and proceeded to meet the demands of rightwing military officers and the hidebound oligarchy. The lack of a strong mobilizing capacity and inadequate communication with the popular sectors they represent have undermined the ability of UASP and the labor movement to pressure the government to fulfill agreements and meet popular demands. The utter failure of a general strike called by UNSITRAGUA in August 1988 highlighted the weak state of the popular movement.

Although the popular movement became an important presence in the late 1980s, particularly in light of the repression it faced, it did not approach the degree of popular organizing experienced in the 1970s. Nonetheless, UASP did create a base of unity from which a resurgent popular movement could challenge the civilian government. It set the tone of resistance by demanding that the government honor its commitments to respect human rights and meet the basic needs of the country's poor majority.

The transition to civilian rule provided the popular sectors with a political opening to show their concern about such matters as low wages, forced service in civil patrols, landlessness, and human rights violations. In a change from the 1970s and early 1980s, marches and demonstrations were again permitted. But the ability of the popular organizations to expand this movement was severely limited by the still palpable atmosphere of repression and the marginalization of the popular sectors from the country's economic, political, and military power structures.

Increasingly during the late 1980s those who dared to join the struggle for social change were killed or disappeared. Students, peasant activists, unionists, journalists, and community organizers became victims of a new scourge of anti-popular terrorism. Nevertheless, the popular movement courageously pushed forward. There have been, however, few tangible victories—other than the continued determination to stand up to the oligarchs, generals, and politicians. When the unions and popular coalitions sat down to negotiate accords with the government and private sector, the resulting accords were routinely violated. And when they went out on strike or dared to confront directly the perpetrators of human rights abuses, they were brutally repressed.

The popular movement in Guatemala has been cut off from its history by decades of systematic repression. As new leaders rise, they are killed or exiled. Not only has the popular movement suffered from the elimination of its most experienced leaders but it has also been isolated from its base of support. Guatemalans have internalized the long campaign of terror and fear the consequences of any form of organizing. Nevertheless, deepening poverty, the hunger of their children, the indignity of living without rights, and the courage of selfless activists have kept the movement alive.

The isolation of the popular movement from the political parties, the guerrilla movement, and the peace process has contributed to its weak presence. Remarkably few links exist between the popular organizations and the political parties, and their demands have not found a place in the electoral arena despite the patent decline in the country's socioeconomic conditions. Both the armed and popular movements suffer from the absence of a strong infrastructure of support and the lack of a well-defined platform of political and economic change. As a result, their efforts only rarely complement one another, keeping both movements relatively weak. Although the popular organizations have certainly supported negotiations to end the war, they have had neither the strength nor the political vision to assert themselves as a principal force in forging peace and developing a new social order.

Outside the country the Guatemalan popular movement includes many exiled organizations such as the Guatemalan Church in Exile, the Guatemalan Democratic Forum (FDG), and the Guatemalan Human Rights Commission (CDHG). This exiled popular movement also includes the organized refugee community in Mexico, a collection of banned journalists, and hundreds of other small Guatemalan groups involved in solidarity and education work.

Within the country but outside the overt popular movement are the Communities of Population in Resistance (CPR), which are entire communities of displaced families and returned refugees operating in clandestinity. Associated with the URNG guerrilla coalition, these communities offer a cooperative and revolutionary alternative to the dominant forms of rural social organization. (See Refugees)

Labor and Unions

Enlarged photographs of eight murdered unionists adorn the walls of the labor union representing workers at the Coca-Cola bottling plant in Guatemala City.[1] These heroes are among hundreds that have fallen victim to death squads and military repression since 1954. Union activists, however, need no reminder that union organizing is a life-threatening activity. While wholesale murders of union organizers waned during the later part of the 1980s, the disappearance and death of labor activists was still not uncommon.[2]

Being a worker in Guatemala means living on survival's edge. The daily minimum wage for an agricultural worker is $1.20 while other workers are supposed to receive at least $1.70. Most workers do not, however, collect even this bare minimum — which is far below the $5.00 a day that a family requires to meet its basic needs. Yet many Guatemalans who do work for these substandard wages count themselves among the fortunate, mindful of the high unemployment rate.

Few Guatemalan workers are organized into unions. About 4 percent of the workforce belong to unions — a rate which, while low, is the highest experienced in Guatemala since before the 1954 coup when as many as a third of the workers were organized. Repression is the main obstacle to labor organizing, but it is not the only one. An antiquated Labor Code, an unresponsive Ministry of Labor, the large pool of cheap labor, and the growth of *solidarista* associations are among the varied impediments faced by unions.[3]

Nonetheless, the Guatemalan labor movement steadily intensified in the 1980s, especially since 1983 when labor organizing was once again officially permitted. The main growth occurred among government and municipal employees, whose right to organize was recognized for the first time in 1986.[4] Continued repression and union-breaking tactics have slowed the movement's advance in the private sector. In the face of strikes and occupations by unions, numerous factories have simply closed, reopening with newly hired employees who are included in management-sponsored *solidarista* associations. Private companies, especially after the May 1988 coup attempt, have been able to rely on ready police support. In contrast, unions find that neither the police nor Ministry of Labor will act to protect workers' rights or to enforce court decisions favorable to the workers.

Among the main demands of the labor movement in the late 1980s were: an increase in the minimum wage to 10 *quetzales* a day (about $3.70) from the 1989 minimum of 4.20 *quetzales*; a price freeze on basic goods;

a revision of the Labor Code; government rejection of petitions by *solidarista* associations for legal status as worker representatives.[5]

At the beginning of the 1990s the labor movement encompassed three major confederations, a smaller one formed in late 1988, various independent unions, and a few peasant associations. Unions were further divided into different coalitions of the broader popular movement. The two popular alliances are UASP and COSU (Unitary Union Coordinator), the latter having been formed in 1988 by the Christian Democratic CGTG labor federation as a pro-government counterpart of UASP. The main confederations and unions are as follows:

The **Confederation of Guatemalan Trade Union Unity (CUSG)** originated on May Day 1983 with the official blessing of the Ríos Montt government. A principal reason for its founding was to demonstrate that Guatemala qualified in terms of labor rights for the benefits of the Caribbean Basin Initiative. The union's main figures are Juan Francisco Alfaro Mijanos and his brother Antonio. Francisco Alfaro, a lawyer, was a member of the Council of State during the Ríos Montt regime and makes no secret of his future political ambitions.

Internationally, CUSG is associated with the International Confederation of Free Trade Unions (ICFTU) and regionally it relates to the Interamerican Regional Organization of Workers (ORIT). Its main affiliation, however, is with the American Institute for Free Labor Development (AIFLD), the principal source of its funding. AIFLD, in turn, receives its funding from the U.S. Agency for International Development (AID) and the United States Information Agency (USIA). CUSG shares the center-right social democratic politics of AIFLD, an associate of the AFL-CIO labor confederation in the United States.

CUSG, the best-financed confederation in Guatemala, offers instruction in "free trade union" principles at local and U.S. workshops to any Guatemalan unionist willing to attend. Its base is mostly among rural associations formed to receive inexpensive agricultural inputs and to benefit from community development projects sponsored by AIFLD and AID.[6] Despite its clear pro-U.S. and anti-leftist orientation, CUSG joined the UASP popular coalition in 1987. This unlikely association of the AIFLD-sponsored confederation with the more progressive UNSITRAGUA confederation in UASP was perceived in labor circles as an opportunity to give Francisco Alfaro a wider popular base than he could achieve through the many phantom unions that constitute CUSG.[7] By 1989 Alfaro had become a dominant voice in UASP. His presence contributed to the continuing lack of a coherent, progressive, and united leadership in the popular movement.

In mid-1990 CUSG dropped out of the UASP popular coalition and angered other labor confederations by throwing its support behind the center-right UCN party. It was thought likely that Alfaro himself would become a UCN candidate for a congressional seat. This politicking by CUSG may jeopardize the confederation's association with AIFLD.

The **Union of Guatemalan Workers (UNSITRAGUA)** was founded in February 1985 and is identified with the most progressive sectors of the labor and popular movement. Many of the nearly 25 unions that form UNSITRAGUA were previously affiliated with the National Committee of Trade Union Unity (CNUS), which disintegrated under the repression of the Lucas García regime. UNSITRAGUA is not affiliated with any international or regional confederations.

Among its strongest unions have been Central American Glass Company Workers Union (STICAVISA), Coca-Cola Bottling Company Trade Union (STECSA), and San Carlos University Workers Union (STUSC). UNSITRAGUA is concentrated in the industrial sector and secondarily in banking and services, with little outreach in the public sector. Yet the influence of UNSITRAGUA extends beyond the confederated unions. As the most progressive confederation, it has opened up political space for all unions. In its battles to defend the rights and demands of associated unions in the private sector, UNSITRAGUA suffered numerous defeats, leaving it weak and with little mobilizing ability among the private-sector trade unions. Beginning in 1988 UNSITRAGUA provided critical institutional support for the struggles of the CUC farmworkers organizations.

Unable to force management to the bargaining table through strikes, unions associated with UNSITRAGUA have resorted to plant occupations. Such an occupation by the Coca-Cola workers in 1984 was brought to a successful conclusion largely because of broad international support for the determined union members. Subsequent occupations have not met with the same success. The seven-month occupation of the Acumuladores Víctor factory ended in a union defeat in late 1987 when the company fired union members, reorganized under a new name, and hired non-union employees. After an eight-month occupation of the Lunafil textile factory in 1988 an accord was reached, but the union was decimated and now barely functions. In June 1990 the government ended the four-month occupation of the CAVISA glass factory by sending in riot police to remove the protesting workers.[8]

The **General Confederation of Guatemalan Workers (CGTG)**, a Christian Democratic labor confederation, was formally established in April 1986 although it had been in the works since 1982. Based largely on public-sector unions, CGTG is closely tied to the Christian Democratic government. Its financial support comes from the Latin American Confederation of Workers (CLAT) and the Konrad Adenauer Foundation of West Germany. The leading figure within CGTG has been Julio Celso de León, a longtime Social Christian labor leader who was replaced in late 1988 by José Pinzón, a CLAT organizer from Costa Rica. Celso de León, who became an associate of the ASIES think tank, has since joined the PSD political party along with ASIES associate Héctor Rosada. Aside from its base among some state institutions, CGTG has some private-sector unions, including those that represent the workers of *La Prensa Libre* and the Kern's food-processing company. Intense competition exists between CGTG and CUSG, neither of which will enter a labor coalition to which the other belongs. CGTG is the leading element of the Unitary Union Coordinator (COSU), created in 1988 as the pro-government counterbalance to UASP.

Formerly one of the main union federations within CUSG, the **Central Federation of Guatemalan Workers (FECETRAG)** and its leader, Ismael Barrios, broke with CUSG to form its own confederation in late 1988. A longtime Social Christian leader, Barrios developed political and personal differences with the Alfaro brothers. FECETRAG has been outspoken in its condemnation of UASP and UNSITRAGUA, which it claims have been infiltrated by insurgents and foreigners. It is a member of the pro-government COSU coalition.[9]

Formed in 1969, the **Bank and Insurance Workers Federation (FESEBS)** includes 19 unions, several of which joined the federation after 1986, when state financial workers began to organize. FESEBS claims to represent 80 percent of the banking sector, although it includes only one insurance union. Its present focus is on organizing financing companies. In 1988, it began a unionization drive at the Army Bank, and was rewarded with intense repression, exemplified when, in October 1988, a FESEBS leader, Carlos Godoy, was gunned down during the thick of the organizing. FESEBS is a member of UASP.

The **National Electric Workers Union (STINDE)** is probably the largest and best organized union in Guatemala. Created in 1985 as the union of the National Electrification Institute, STINDE has been the repeated target of repression. Three STINDE leaders were forced to flee the country during a 1988 strike. STINDE is a member of UASP.

Public-sector employees are, in general, better organized than their counterparts in the private sector. During the Christian Democratic government, they have been at the forefront of the labor movement. Like STINDE, others have joined the UASP coalition, including the **National**

Teachers Union (STEG) and the National Federation of State Workers Unions (FENASTEG). A nationwide strike in mid-1989 by teachers and postal workers demonstrated the new-found power, unity, and militancy of the organized public-sector employees. The public-sector unions have been widely criticized for focusing too narrowly on their own economic goals rather than using their comparatively privileged position to demand economic changes that would benefit the entire working class and other poor sectors.

In addition to CUC, other peasant organizations emerged in the 1980s. Some formed to demand land from the Christian Democratic government, the most prominent of which was the Pro-Land movement led by Padre Andrés Girón. Other peasant organizations include the Highland Campesino Committee (CCDA), Campesino Union of the South (UCS), and the Rural Workers Central (CTC). In 1988 the Worker and Peasant Federation (FESOC) formed as a pro-government organization, with apparent connections to CGTG. For their part, CUSG also sponsors various rural associations, though these are mostly self-help community organizations rather than actual unions.

Solidarismo: Labor/Owner Cooperation

The 1980s saw the growth of worker groups called *solidarista* associations. *Solidarismo* is a philosophy of labor/ownership formulated in Costa Rica in 1947, where it has received important support from the Catholic church, big business, and more recently AID. In practice, *solidarismo* takes the form of financial associations in which workers and businesses form credit cooperatives, food services for workers, and investment projects. Most of the capital used for these projects comes from employee savings and the investment by the company owner of severance pay due to each worker. It is supported by businesses as an alternative to class confrontation, unionism, and collective bargaining.

Solidarismo first appeared in Guatemala in 1963. At the behest of business owners, Alvaro Portela, a *solidarista* organizer, helped form the first *solidarista* association in the department of Quiché. The movement did not, however, experience rapid growth until 1983 with the founding of the Guatemalan Solidarista Union. By the end of the decade *solidarismo* boasted 280 associations with some 80,000 members.[10]

An ever-growing and enthusiastic portion of the Guatemalan private sector regards *solidarismo* as a modern response to the threat of unionization. Rather than simply repressing union activists, businesses can now promote the alternative of *solidarismo*. Its origins can be traced to the emphasis placed by the Catholic church on class cooperation rather than class conflict. Instead of competing for the fruits of their labor, workers and their employer form a *solidarista* association with the declared objective of pooling resources for their mutual benefit.

Promoted by U.S. and local corporations and financially backed by AID, *solidarismo* is expanding throughout Central America from its base in Costa Rica.[11] Leading the campaign are a group of Guatemalan businessmen and U.S. consultants, many of whom are closely associated with the Management Association of Guatemala (AGG). They include Enrique and Ricardo Arenas, owners of the La Perla *finca* in Ixcán; José Rolz, owner of the CONAPEL paper mill, and Joseph Recinos, managing director of the Equity Expansion consulting firm. *Solidarista* associations are active in most economic sectors, but are concentrated (40 percent) in the agricultural sector. At least two U.S. transnationals, RJ Reynolds/Del Monte and Ramada Inns, sponsor *solidarista* associations.[12]

In Guatemala, *solidarismo* is being promoted not only to counteract unions but also by the army and landowners to combat rural unrest. The Arenas brothers, directors of the national *solidarista* council, installed an association on their coffee estate, La Perla, in northern Quiché. The La Perla Solidarista Association claims that it has armed its members to defend the estate against leftist insurgents and that the workers themselves have forgone wage hikes so that the association could purchase more weapons. In 1987 the association helped build a 12-kilometer road in this conflictive area, for which the army gave it a plaque noting its appreciation. A *solidarista* association has also been installed in the Las Minas antimony mine in Huehuetenango, a long-time hotbed of labor unrest.

A trait that distinguishes *solidarismo* in Guatemala is its attempt to establish employee stock-ownership plans (ESOP). Such plans were promoted by Joseph Recinos, who (in addition to directing a consulting firm that advocates privatization of state corporations) was a counselor to the U.S. Presidential Task Force on Project Economic Justice in Central America, headed by Ambassador J. William Middendorf (a member of the rightwing Santa Fe Committee).[13] The ESOP concept proposed by Recinos represents the most advanced stage of *solidarismo* and is in place in only a few businesses in Central America. For the most part, *solidarista* associations do little more than sponsor credit unions and other employee services, and at their more advanced stage may form associated businesses to do contract work for the mother company.

Schools and Students

Education is a privilege in Guatemala. With a 50 percent rate of literacy, Guatemala is the least-educated society in Central America. Among children ages 7 to 14, four of every ten do not attend school. Of those who do attend, only 20 percent finish the sixth grade. It is estimated that by the early 1990s, fewer than 40 percent of Guatemalans will be literate.

The University of San Carlos (USAC), the national university, has long enjoyed a reputation as one of the best universities in Latin America. Founded in 1676 by Dominican priests, it was the first (and, until the 1800s, the only) university in Central America. The university has served as a vanguard and barometer of the popular movement, and has accordingly been a prime target of government repression. Like many other Latin American universities, it functions as an autonomous institution and is constitutionally entitled to 5 percent of the government annual budget.

USAC's history of social activism began in 1944 when its students, professors, and workers were strong supporters of the junta that overthrew dictator Jorge Ubico. By the end of that ten-year window of democracy, USAC had evolved into a center of opposition to the Arbenz government, law professors and students publishing strong denunciations of the government's agrarian-reform program, claiming that it violated the property rights of the expropriated landowners. Since 1954, however, USAC has been a leading source of leftist and anti-military criticism.

In the 1960s many students graduated directly from youth clubs and political discussion groups into the ranks of the guerrillas. A leftist critique continued to dominate student thinking at USAC during the 1970s, a time when its academic prestige peaked; but the repression of USAC professors and students plunged the university into academic decline. The violence reached its zenith between 1980 and 1982 during the Lucas García regime, when hundreds of students and professors were killed. As a result of this repression, the nature and quality of instruction at USAC changed dramatically. Courses that involved social criticism were dropped from the curriculum, and many of the best professors were either killed or forced into exile. Progressive university rectors and deans were replaced with conservative, less academically qualified ones.

Student Movement Revives

After 1983 the student movement, decimated during the Lucas García years, gradually came back to life. The Guatemala Association of University Students "Oliverio Casteñeda de León" (AEU), the elected student organization, is attempting to reclaim its former role in the popular movement. Founded in 1920, AEU now includes the name of an assassinated student leader in its full designation. A wall mural on the USAC campus, which commemorates the 1978 murder of Oliverio Casteñeda, admonishes: "You can massacre our leaders, but as long as the people exist, there will be revolution."

Dating back to 1898, the *Huelga de Dolores* has been one of the main manifestations of student dissent in Guatemala. During the week of Palm Sunday, students organize parades in Guatemala City, Quezaltenango, and other cities, which, while part student exuberance, also include an element of biting anti-government criticism. Until 1980, the military refrained from cracking down on this customary release of student energy and protest, but under Lucas García, not even the *Huelga de Dolores* was safe from the death squads. In the late 1980s, the *Huelga de Dolores* grew increasingly bold in its critique of the army and Cerezo government. This is seen most clearly in the clandestine paper *Don't Tempt Us*, published by the *Huelga de Dolores* organizing committee, which includes revolutionary poems and analysis in addition to the sarcastic humor so characteristic of the *Huelga de Dolores* tradition.

Being a student activist, however, entails more than this yearly display of antics. It is a risky undertaking, as the elaborate security measures adopted by AEU testify. The security checks and system of unspecified meeting places is a response to a frightening history of persecution of AEU leaders. The disappearance of members of AEU's executive committee in 1984 forced the organization underground. In 1987 its executive secretary was murdered. Despite the repression, AEU emerged from the shadows in 1988 and joined the UASP popular coalition. AEU activism encompasses economic-justice issues, human rights concerns, labor solidarity, and student issues. On the USAC campus, AEU provides critical support for the workers' union, while aggressively demanding better quality education and more socially relevant studies. In 1988 it stood firmly behind a strike by secondary students who had organized to gain better school facilities and an increased education budget.

The new student activism, however, was met by renewed repression. In March 1989, the entire AEU government council received death threats, with repression against student activists reaching a new peak in August 1989 when 11 students were disappeared. By September 1989 only three of the 16 members of the AEU directorate remained, the others having been killed, disappeared, exiled, or in hiding.

The Private Alternative to USAC

Prior to 1961 USAC was the country's only university. Between 1961 and 1971, however, four new private universities were established. The Rafael Landívar University, founded in 1961, is administered by the Jesuits. In contrast to Jesuit-run universities in El Salvador and Nicaragua, the Landívar University exerts a conservative influence in Guatemalan academia. The Mariano Gálvez University, founded in 1966, was established as an evangelical college although it now professes to be nonsectarian. The University of the Valley, founded in 1966, is an outgrowth of the American School of Guatemala, and currently benefits from regular allocations of U.S. economic aid. In 1971 the Francisco Marroquín University was founded to spread neoliberal economic thinking and neoconservative politics in Guatemala. This conservative and well-heeled university also benefits from several U.S. economic-aid programs.

The rise of the private universities did not decrease enrollment in USAC but the establishment of these private universities has reduced the commitment of the national elite to maintain USAC as a source of quality higher education. The private universities serve to train a professional class in an academic atmosphere free of the leftist influence seen at USAC. While an expanded private role in higher education is a more recent trend, secondary education has long been dominated by private institutions. Of 459 secondary schools, the 83 percent that are private serve 55 percent of the student population.[14] Another force in the privatization of education is the business elite which has recently begun, with U.S. government assistance, to publish and distribute textbooks promoting capitalist ideology. The Chamber of Industry, for example, distributes a Basic School Kit.

Communications Media

By some very narrow standards, Guatemala is said to have a free press. In one 1988 international study, Guatemala was found to have little or no press restrictions and was ranked in the highest of eight categories.[15] There is no censorship board in Guatemala, no press licensing, and the country's leading paper is even called *La Prensa Libre* ("Free Press") — but journalists are disappeared and news outlets are ransacked and firebombed by masked men.

During the first several years of the Cerezo government there were signs that the country was indeed increasing its press freedoms after years of military rule. In early 1988 two new magazines were established: *Crónica*, a weekly magazine in the style of *Newsweek* and *Time*, and the short-lived *La Epoca*, which featured investigative reporting and critical political analysis. Television news took on new life, and reporters could travel to any region of the country without government permission.

By mid-1988, however, hopes for increasing press freedom in Guatemala came crashing down. In June 1988, heavily armed men broke into the *La Epoca* offices, burglarized it, and then firebombed it. Also destroyed was the office of the news agency ACEN-SIAG (closely associated with *La Epoca*). Shortly before this attack on the social-democratic *La Epoca*, correspondents for the Cuban Prensa Latina and the Soviet Tass news agencies were forced to leave the country after receiving death threats. The home of the Tass correspondent was also firebombed. In the same period, the two leading television news programs were terminated, at least one by direct government behest. At the same time that the ultra-right *Aquí el Mundo* television news program was shut down, the *El País* weekly newspaper, also directed by Mario David García, disappeared from the streets.

For many close observers of Guatemala, the forced closing of *La Epoca* was inevitable given the restricted nature of journalism in the country. Others saw the paper as the "litmus test" of democratic freedoms under the new civilian government. While there was no official censorship under the civilian government, a system of self-censorship reigned that *La Epoca* blatantly violated. In Guatemala, as in many other countries, reporters and editors do not criticize the military or engage in investigative reporting that would challenge established power structures. For the most part, these restrictions are understood and self-imposed. But they exist within the context of a highly repressive society, and have been reinforced by death threats, assassinations, and bomb blasts.

During the 1970s, 49 journalists were kidnapped or murdered. One of these was the popular radio commentator Mario Monterrose Armas, who was gunned to death after criticizing the military government for election fraud. Repression of journalists continued during the the 1980s, during which some four-dozen journalists were forced to flee the country.[16]

The nature and quality of reporting in Guatemala is also determined by the low wages received by journalists. To supplement their low pay, journalists rely on bribes and other forms of payment for service rendered. This system, which is also common in other Central American countries, operates according to the *"fafa"* law. In his 1979 book, *The Business of the Press*, Mario Carpio Nicolle explained that the law of *fafa* (apparently a bastardization of the word "half") dictates that a journalist receives at least half his income from bribes and fees. A reporter or editor, then, will often write or print a story only if a proper payment is forthcoming. The government's Ministry of Public Relations is usually the main source of these bribes.

To illustrate how the system works, Carpio Nicolle related a story in which the government instructed a journalist to write a front-page article on the government's 500,000-tree reforestation plan, for which he would get 500 *quetzales*. When the government gave him only 50 *quetzales*, the reporter wrote a story about 50,000 trees the government was planting. Ten years later, Carpio Nicolle said that the *fafa* system had changed little.

Journalists have tried to organize to increase their independence and to improve the poor quality of Guatemalan journalism. During the 1970s salaried journalists formed the Union of Workers of the Social Communications Media (SIMCOS). The union was eventually crushed and its leaders driven into exile by the Lucas García regime.[17] After the demise of SIMCOS, the Association of Democratic Journalists of Guatemala (APDG) formed also in exile. Within Guatemala, a press employee can choose between the independent Journalistic Association of Guatemala (APG), the Guatemalan Chamber of Journalists (CGP) which has close links with the government and army, or the conservative National Press Circle (CNP). Commenting on the current state of journalism in Guatemala, an editor for the newsmagazine *Crónica* quipped that most reporters are simply "tape machines with legs."[18]

The Daily News

The press became increasingly concentrated during the 1980s. Five daily newspapers —*El Nuevo Diario, Impacto, La Razón, La Nación,* and *El Imparcial* — went out of business, some for business reasons, others for political ones. *El Imparcial,* for example, died mostly of old age after 63 years of publishing. The aging daily simply did not keep pace with changing trends and technology in the newspaper business. A sixth daily, *La Palabra,* was backed by evangelical churches and lasted three years (1983-1986).

Today, Guatemala has only two major daily newspapers —*La Prensa Libre* and *El Gráfico* — with two smaller daily papers, *La Hora* and the recently established *Siglo Veinitiuno.* There is also a government daily, *Diario de Centro América,* which has traditionally simply reproduced government notices and decrees. Under the direction of Carmen Escribano de León (wife of de León Schlotter), *Diario de Centro América* became a more respectable newspaper with a greater circulation. The two leading dailies have become bitter enemies of the Christian Democratic government, *La Prensa Libre* more over ideology, while *El Gráfico* for purely political reasons. Shallow reporting, bad writing, and unattractive layout characterize both papers. News agency reports are usually published in their entirety rather than being integrated into one report by a foreign editor. As a result, it is not uncommon to find two agency reports with essentially the same news appearing side by side. Local death and tragedy dominate the headlines, further contributing to the atmosphere of fear and terror that dominates the country.

La Prensa Libre, founded in 1951, is the undisputed leading daily newspaper. An ultra-right publication, *La Prensa Libre* (70,000 circulation) is owned by five families. Pedro Julio García is the current director, and another owner is Tere Bolaños de Zarco, the widow of a well-known Guatemalan journalist who was assassinated in 1978.[19] Her son, José Eduardo Zarco Bolaños, is one of the newspaper's leading columnists. Other important figures are Alvaro Contreras Vélez and Marco Sandoval Figueroa. The paper is closely allied with the military and the elite business community, and is known to have a military intelligence officer on staff. Virulently anti-government, *La Prensa Libre* refuses to publish government press releases. The paper maintains close links with the Nicaraguan contras, and it prohibits its reporters from interviewing political dissidents such as Padre Andrés Girón or GAM's Nineth García.

El Gráfico, founded in 1963, is owned by the director of the National Center Union (UCN) political party, Jorge Carpio Nicolle. Party politics and the news mix freely in *El Gráfico*, which serves as the voice of the UCN. Like *La Prensa Libre*, *El Gráfico* (circulation 60,000) is clearly opposed to the Christian Democratic government. It propagates a rightwing ideology less extremist than its competitor. The paper, which began as a sports weekly, is 65 percent advertising. At one time, *El Gráfico* also published a news magazine for intellectuals called *La Razón*, but has since dropped its pretensions to be anything other than a business venture and political instrument for the UCN. Columnist Jorge Palmieri, who served as Ambassador to Mexico during the Lucas García regime, serves as a mouthpiece for CACIF, which pays him for his services. Palmieri, a rightist, has a reputation for making unsubstantiated assertions. In mid-1989, Palmieri left *El Gráfico* and now writes for the weekly *7 Días*.

La Hora, established in 1944, is owned by the Marroquín family. Its founder, Clemente Marroquín Rojas, served as vice-president during the government of Julio Méndez Montenegro (1966-1970). Like the other dailies, *La Hora* owns its own press. Because of its small circulation (about 5,000) and its lack of advertising, it is a losing business proposition. *La*

Hora is published not to make money but for reasons of prestige and political ambition by the Marroquín family. Shortly after the muckraking *La Epoca* was bombed, the Marroquíns began publishing a new weekly called *7 Días* as a less intrepid version of the former publication. Its director is Gonzalo Marroquín, the former owner and director of the *Siete Días* television news program.

Joining *La Hora* in early 1990 was the new morning daily *Siglo Veintiuno*, distinguished by its professional appearance and reporting, as well as by its pluralistic approach. On its board sit members of the influential Castillo and Toriello families. The increasing impact of *Siglo Veintiuno* could be measured by the defensive and negative commentary its appearance elicited from its competitors.

The only other major source of written news in Guatemala is *Crónica*, a weekly magazine that began publishing in early 1988. A slick and expensive magazine, *Crónica* (circulation 10,000) quickly attracted attention because of the superior quality of its writing and graphic presentation. The magazine's owners and directors represent the most modern and intelligent elements of the private sector. These include: Francisco Pérez de Antón (a Spanish-born businessman with wide cultural and intellectual interests who is associated with the CAEM business chamber and is an owner of the Pollo Campero fast-food chain); Juan Fernando Quezada Toruño (an important lawyer and brother of Bishop Quezada Toruño), Rodolfo Gutiérrez Machado (an investor and well-known publicity agent), and Juan Caso Fanjul (a Spanish-born investor). In mid-1989, the magazine was torn by internal strife when its director, Richard Aitkenhead Castillo (former president of the Association of Business Managers and a leading force behind the defunct *Siete Días* television news program), along with three editors left the publication because owner Pérez de Antón decided that Aitkenhead was gaining too much influence. Since then *Crónica* has lost much of its stylistic flair.

The Electronic Media

Radio reaches more Guatemalans than any other medium. Radio Fabulosa, the country's most influential station, boasts a chain of affiliated stations throughout the country. Altogether, some one hundred radio stations operate in Guatemala. Virtually all radio news is produced by *radioperiódicos*, independent news services that buy time on individual stations. There is less military, government, or private-sector control over radio than any other media, although self-censorship reigns here as well. In the last several years, there has been a surge in evangelical radio programming. In 1987 the airwaves in Guatemala were infiltrated by a

Friday afternoon short-wave program, *La Voz Popular* (The Popular Voice), broadcast by the UNRG guerrillas from unknown locations. Now broadcast twice weekly, the URNG radio program has been blocked in many locations by expensive army jamming efforts.

The government, through its National Broadcasting Committee, grants broadcasting rights to four private television stations. In addition, there is one government-owned channel. Recently, cable television has burgeoned, primarily in Guatemala City. There are some 50,000 cable subscribers, virtually all of whom receive their cable television from small private companies that illegally receive satellite transmissions from U.S. cable companies. A 1989 survey by the ACEN-SIAG news agency revealed that 78 percent of the programming on the country's five channels is foreign-produced.[20]

Two issues — foreign ownership of television stations and control over television news — surfaced in 1988 when two television news programs were forced off the air.[21] In the case of Channel 3, the government in May 1988 notified its owner, Radio-Television Guatemala, that it was canceling its broadcasting privileges, letting it know unofficially that the problem was not with the station itself but with *Aquí El Mundo* (Here's the World), the separately owned and operated news program. While the station denounced the order, it also announced that it was canceling its contract with *Aquí El Mundo*.

Founded in 1976, *Aquí El Mundo* was Guatemala's first modern news program, interspersing live news reports with commentary. Its abrasive, extreme rightwing politics captured the bulk of the TV audience until the *Siete Días* program on Channel 7 captured the number one spot in 1987. The immediate reason for the government's move against *Aquí El Mundo* was its favorable coverage of and cheerleading for the attempted military coup of May 11, 1988. For the government (and the army), *Aquí El Mundo* had no place in the "new democracy." Many of the personnel formerly associated with *Aquí El Mundo* plan a new television news-analysis program to be called *TV Noticias*.

About the same time, *Siete Días* also left the air. Over the previous year, disputes had arisen between the program's majority owner, Gonzalo Marroquín, and the ownership of Channel 7. Marroquín divulged that financial control of both Channel 3 and Channel 7 was held by Mexicans. He called upon the National Congress to pass a law prohibiting foreigners from enjoying broadcasting privileges in Guatemala. Further complicating the dispute were the public friendships that had developed between President Cerezo and his Foreign Minister Alfonso Cabrera, and Remigio Angel González y González, the Mexican who owned the station through his wife. It is widely believed that the termination of the popular *Siete Días* was due in large part to government pressure, in hopes of creating another news program beholden to the Christian Democratic party. *Siete Días* was replaced by the less professional *Noti-7* program.

The two other channels, 11 and 13, are owned, at least in part, by Honduran investors. Channel 11's news program is *Teleprensa*, owned by José Elías Tárano. The army station, Channel 5, airs many cultural programs as well as religious presentations like *El Club 700* produced by Pat Robertson's Christian Broadcasting Network. CNN news is broadcast on Channels 3 (in Spanish) and 13 (in English). The government's news program, *Hoy Lo Más Importante*, is aired on all stations. There is a new UHF channel, Channel 25, which airs mostly music videos but does have its own conservative news program. Channel 21 is the evangelical station.

The United States Information Service (USIS) exercises important influence on the media through its many media services. Daily press bulletins are distributed to all major newspapers, television, and radio news programs. Programs produced by the Voice of America (VOA) and the local USIS mission are fed to 41 radio stations. In addition, VOA editorials reach 10 radio news programs broadcast on 60 stations. USIS also produced a weekly 30-minute news feature program and a daily recorded commentary program carried by 20 stations. USIS also produces and distributes a wide range of television programs, including the Worldnet service.[22] Through a new AID program, Guatemalan journalists are brought to the United States for cultural and professional education.

The State of Health

Guatemala is often found at the top of regional lists. Commonly considered the most beautiful country in Central America, it has long been regarded as the most repressive. It is the most populous nation and also the richest in terms of natural resources. Excluding Panama, it is the wealthiest country in terms of aggregate gross national product. At the same time, though, Guatemalans are the most deprived and least healthy citizens on the isthmus. According to a 1982 UNICEF study, Guatemala has the lowest "physical quality of life" index in Central America, and the third-lowest in Latin America, after Haiti and Bolivia.[23]

So severe and widespread are hunger, malnutrition, and illness in Guatemala that they can only be described as a type of social violence. Even at the height of the counterinsurgency campaign in the early 1980s, more Guatemalans were dying of malnutrition and preventable disease than of political causes. And while there have been fewer political killings in recent years, this background of daily death continues, ever exacerbated.

Guatemala wins the unenviable awards for the highest rates of infant mortality, illiteracy, and malnutrition in the region, while offering the lowest life expectancy, and the least amount spent on health care per person. Only 51 percent of Guatemalans have access to safe water supplies; only 34 percent have regular access to health services.[24] In Guatemala City, half the population has no daily access to a toilet and three of four children under five are malnourished.[25]

The overall averages, as appalling as they are, hide the alarming disparities between Indian and *ladino* health. The life expectancy for non-Indian men is 65 years, and 64 years for non-Indian women. But Indian males can expect to live only 48 years, and Indian women only 47 years.

The two top causes of death in Guatemala are gastrointestinal and respiratory infections, brought on by malnutrition and poor sanitary conditions, stemming primarily from a lack of potable water.[26] A leading cause of death for Guatemalan children is measles due to the large number of unvaccinated children in the country. A government study in 1981 found that 70 percent of the deaths of children under five were due to easily preventable diseases. During a 1986 visit to Guatemala, the regional director of UNICEF addressed this tragedy of preventable death, lamenting: "Guatemala has the worst infant mortality rate in Central America. Every day 115 Guatemalan children under five — that's five children every hour — die from such diseases as diphtheria, whooping cough, tetanus, measles, or polio."[27] Fifteen percent of Guatemalan children suffer from eye diseases, and one of every six afflicted children is blind.[28]

Health care facilities are of notoriously poor quality in Guatemala. Only the wealthy and the military enjoy reasonably good health care. Two government agencies, the Ministry of Public Health and Social Assistance (MSPAS) and the Guatemalan Social Security Institute (IGSS), administer the government's health care budget. While there is a social-security system, it covers only 12 percent of the total population, or one-quarter of the active workforce. But even if a person is covered by social security or does have some income to pay for health care, the country's clinics and hospitals are extremely under-budgeted, under-staffed, and undersupplied. In fact, most rural health posts have no medicines. Guatemala does have a large number of hospital beds when compared with other Central American countries. Yet most of these beds are in private hospitals, beyond the reach of the impoverished majority.

In the 1980s the government's health care budget was repeatedly slashed, even though it was already one of the lowest in the hemisphere at the beginning of the decade. While the public health budget was being cut, the number of patients was increasing. Apparently because of the economic crisis, private clinics are closing down and more sick Guatemalans are now taking their health problems to public hospitals. Budget shortfalls have forced some public hospitals to curtail services simply because they had no funds to clean the laundry or provide drinking water. Workers at one Guatemala City hospital erected a banner explaining: "This is not a strike. There is no budget."

At even the most basic level of preventive vaccination, Guatemala demonstrates little commitment to public health. It has the lowest immunization rate in Latin America—with only one of eight children vaccinated against measles and two of five having received the required dosage of polio and DPT immunization.

Stepping in to fill the health care gap in Guatemala have been numerous foreign humanitarian and religious organizations. But for the most part this source of health care has not been very effective in seriously combating the country's deplorable state of health. One exception is the Maryknoll project in Huehuetenango, which for the last 25 years has been training health care promoters. Like other programs that incorporate a certain degree of community empowerment and popular education, the Maryknoll project was hard hit by counterinsurgency terror as over 160 promoters either fled the country, quit, or were killed from 1981-1989. Another program that has tried to improve the health status of rural Guatemalans through popular education techniques is ACECSA, which is based in Chimaltenango.

Medical workers run great political risk in Guatemala. Doctors, nurses, medical students, and health care promoters are targets for repression. Medical neutrality is not respected by the government, which has failed to ratify the Geneva Conventions on the safety of medical personnel. From 1980 to 1988, there were 125 cases of serious violations of medical neutrality, including the killing and disappearance of medical students, health professionals, and patients (abducted from medical facilities and killed). During this same period, some 500 health promoters were killed or disappeared.[29]

Religion

More than any other Latin American country, Guatemala has become a religious battleground. The country is already one-third evangelical

(Protestant). If present growth rates continue, the major religious persuasion in Guatemala will become evangelical soon after the turn of the century. Alarmed by this trend, Archbishop Próspero Penados del Barrio branded the evangelical movement an imperialist conspiracy to assert U.S. economic and political dominance in the region. Responding in turn, the head of the Evangelical Alliance asserted that the Catholic church is desperately trying to "influence the state and control the population," while keeping alive "idolatry, fetishism, alcoholism, and machoism — all that it defends as 'tradition'."[30]

The Catholic-evangelical contest in Guatemala is more than a battle for souls. Questions about religious persuasion often have a political ring in this country which several years ago had a fervent evangelical as president and where the ruling Christian Democrats have cultivated ties with the Catholic church. During the height of the counterinsurgency frenzy in the highlands, Catholics were identified as subversives while the army considered evangelicals to be firm anticommunists. But aside from the immediate political implications of the evangelical movement, the ongoing religious upheaval is tearing at the social seams of this highly repressed and traditional society, opening the way for deeper social and political changes as yet unforeseen.[31]

The Catholic Church: Power, Tradition, and Change

The Roman Catholic Church is the country's major religious institution. As such, it has played a major role not only in the religious and cultural aspects of Guatemalan life, but also in such diverse areas as politics, community development, social services, and refugee relief. Catholic clerical and lay initiatives have often served as important models for the development programs of many other private organizations and even a few government agencies.

Independence from Spain and the rise of a new economic elite of coffee growers in the 19th century weakened the hold of the Catholic church. When the Liberals seized political power from the Conservatives in 1871, the church suffered a shocking loss of power and prestige. Lands were confiscated, monasteries closed down, and foreign clergy deported. President Justo Rufino Barrios declared religious freedom, and opened up the country to Protestantism.

It was not until the 1930s that the Catholic church recovered a portion of its former prestigious position in society. Under the regime of dictator Jorge Ubico, the church began to exercise some of its previous political influence. In 1944, when Ubico was overthrown by a coalition of progressive army officers and civilians intent on modernizing Guatemala, the church felt that its own social and political power was under attack. During the next ten years, the church and its lay organizations such as Catholic Action joined with the Anti-Communist Party (PUA) and other rightwing organizations to protest the liberalizing and reformist trends of the civilian governments.

The church's anticommunist attacks on the Jacobo Arbenz government contributed to the government's inability to withstand the eventual rightwing military coup. In fact, Archbishop Mariano Rossell personally cooperated in the campaign directed by the Central Intelligence Agency (CIA) to topple the democratically elected government.

The 1954 coup proved to be a blessing for the institutional church. Archbishop Rossell was awarded the Order of Liberation by the new government of Castillo Armas and the Movement for National Liberation (MLN). In turn, the archbishop referred to Castillo Armas as a "legitimate saint." The new regime removed restrictions on church ownership of property, opened the country to foreign clergy, and dropped restrictions in the public schools to religious instruction. For its part, the Catholic church blessed the military government and echoed its anticommunist ideology.

The late 1950s to the early 1960s was a period of revitalization and institutional growth for the Catholic church. After 1954 priests and nuns from all over Europe and North America came to Guatemala as missionaries. Post-World War II prosperity in Europe and the United States, the expulsion of religious orders from China in the 1940s, and the call by the Pope John XXIII for external help to the churches in Latin America all contributed to the influx of foreign Catholic missionaries after 1954. New schools and churches were built, new diocese and missions were opened in previously ignored areas, lay apostolic organizations were created, and church social-assistance programs were substantially expanded.

As in the rest of the world, the Guatemalan Catholic church experienced major internal upheaval in the 1960s. The Vatican Council II in 1962 and the Medellín Bishops' Conference in 1968 jolted clergy and laity alike into reexamining the church's traditional place in society and politics. Even though the national church hierarchy strongly resisted these liberalizing trends, many of the local clergy caught the spirit of change and transmitted that spirit to their parishioners.

Even more catalytic were internal factors that tilted much of the church toward political dissent and support for worker and peasant struggles. For a significant minority of missionary priests and nuns, particularly those working in rural areas, the narrow anticommunist ideology with which they entered Guatemala changed dramatically: first to a focus on developmentalism and self-help measures, and later to a more critical stance and an alliance with those seeking profound social and economic changes.

Through Catholic lay groups like Catholic Action and Delegates of the Word, poor people came together to learn more about the Catholic faith and to discuss community problems. Priests and nuns, often relying on foreign resources, encouraged the formation of savings and loan cooperatives, buying and marketing cooperatives, and the use of fertilizers. Together with the lay groups, they formed campesino training centers, organized literacy campaigns, and spearheaded colonization projects in Ixcán, Petén, and northern Huehuetenango. This developmentalist response ran parallel to and oftentimes overlapped with similar projects sponsored by AID and the Alliance for Progress.

But this developmentalism soon reached its limits. In the process, lay religious leaders became community leaders and were thrust into confrontation with established local and national power structures. Catholic Action leaders, imbued with the "new Catholicism," often broke ranks with traditional Indian spokesmen and leading figures of the *cofradías*. When dealing with land and work issues, they also came face to face with local oligarchs and army officers who used their considerable power to repress cooperatives and other lay organizations spawned by Catholic Action.

Both clergy and laity became increasingly radicalized as the economic elite and the army escalated their repression. Many lay Catholic leaders gradually moved away from the church organizations to form peasant leagues, while others joined guerrilla movements. In the mid-1960s several priests also became guerrilla supporters and were expelled from the country. Repression against the rural church intensified. By the early 1980s, the entire diocese of Quiché was closed and 13 priests had been killed.[32] In 1980 banished priests and nuns formed the Guatemalan Church in Exile, which continues to function and publishes a journal about counterinsurgency, refugees, and repression in Guatemala.

The institutional or hierarchical church was not unaffected by the changes taking place in the rural church, particularly in the highlands. As an institution, the Catholic church is financially and organizationally spread thin. Before the early 1960s the only formal voice of the church was that of the archbishop in Guatemala City. But encouraged by Vatican Council II, bishops, priests, and nuns began forming their own associations, including the Conference of Religious Orders of Guatemala (CONFREGUA) founded in 1961.

Upon Archbishop Rossell's death in 1964, Mario Casariego became the new archbishop in Guatemala and was later honored by the Pope as Central America's first cardinal. Casariego, like his predecessor, was an ardent anticommunist. For almost two decades, until his death in 1983, the politically adept but widely disliked Spanish Casariego strove to maintain the institutional church as a conservative institution that gave no support to the developmentalist and reformist trends that were emerging from the church's rural base. Despite the constant repression and escalating bloodshed by the army, the archbishop's office enjoyed cordial and often friendly relations with the military government and oligarchy.

Although anti-government sentiment did exist among certain sectors of the church, Archbishop Casariego managed to keep the institutional church largely aligned with the government and military. In spite of Casariego, the Guatemalan bishops did circulate several progressive communiques and pastorals during his tenure. Upon Casariego's death, the military paid its respects at a ceremony in the National Palace. During the ceremony, General Héctor Mario López Fuentes eulogized, "Until his death, [Casariego] was the spiritual guide of many army officers and the confessor of the majority and he was considered the religious guide of the military institution with which he was always identified."

Following the death of Casariego in 1983, the church became a more unified institution under Archbishop Próspero Penados del Barrio. In the wake of intense persecution of the rural church in the highlands and charges from the military that the church was breeding revolution, a healing process began. With the ouster of Ríos Montt—who had granted evangelical sects a prominent place in Guatemalan society—the Catholic church hierarchy could breathe more easily. The election of a Christian Democratic president two years later also helped the church to recover its strength and influence.

To a large degree, the moderate, developmentalist approach of the Christian Democratic government matched the institutional church's own social and political ideology. The church, like the Christian Democratic Party, has regarded its social message as a third way between communism and unbridled capitalism. By the third year of the Cerezo government, the Catholic bishops grew more insistent that social reforms be instituted to improve the lot of the poor, whose circumstances were worsening rather than improving under the Christian Democrats.

The church under Penados del Barrio moved sharply away from the conservatism of the Casariego years. The new social voice of the institutional church became obvious with the March 1988 release of the pastoral letter "The Cry for Land." The pastoral letter's call for land distribution sorely angered the national elite, simultaneously lifting hopes among the poor that the church would become an ally in the struggle for justice. A year later, the Bishops' Conference issued another strong statement, called the Declaration of Cobán, concerning the country's deplorable economic, and social conditions. The bishops charged that the country's "economic structure increases the wealth of the privileged sector [while making] the majority of Guatemalans even poorer." Furthermore, they noted that "more than a few Guatemalans have lost their faith in the possibility of an authentic democratic process."[33] Still stronger was the Declaration of January 1990 which criticized the army. The joint documents of the country's Bishops' Conference have been the most progressive in Central America in recent years.[34]

This voice of social criticism is welcome in a country where so many other voices have been silenced. The prophetic or denunciatory voice of the church is present, but remains a minor part of the church's social response. The church's more socially committed and activist elements have been either forced out of the country or isolated within the institution. Lay organizations like the Delegates of the Word continue to exist but their work is largely limited to strictly pastoral functions. While the Bishops' Conference has in recent years become an important and largely unified source of social criticism, it remains to be seen to what degree the institutional church hierarchy will encourage and defend increased social activism by its own clergy and laity.

Repression of the Catholic church escalated in 1989. Lay workers, nuns, parish priests, and Archbishop Próspero Penados have all received death threats because of their involvement in national reconciliation efforts. In late October a Maryknoll nun was forced to leave the country after a death threat. The following month an Ursuline sister was kidnapped, sexually abused, and tortured by government security forces, and a member of the Archdiocesan Lay Council was murdered. Also in late 1989 the army base in Chiquimula issued orders that all priests working in that eastern region were to be interrogated by army personnel.[35]

As an institution, the Catholic church is weak, poor, and dependent. Over two-thirds of its clerics are still foreigners. The church is largely centered in major urban areas, with about one-third of the total clergy based in Guatemala City. For the most part, the priests and nuns are conservative, both theologically and politically. At the same time, the church has remained isolated from popular movements and organizations, many of which are led by those who received their first social formation by activist clergy.

In its precarious state, the church is doing little community development organizing and campesino training, relying instead on handout programs. A countervailing trend is the *inserción* (insertion) movement of many religious orders, who are inserting their priests and nuns in poor *barrios* where they live and do pastoral work. While the church hierarchy has repeatedly declined to incorporate a human rights office into the institution, the activist clergy may take up this challenge on their own. CONFREGUA has plans for a Multiple Services Office, possibly including a human rights branch. If the plan goes through, a tenacious ally would be the Monsignor Romero Group, a small committee of Catholic university students that has worked with GAM. Beginning in late 1988, the Romero Group joined with several evangelical groups in an ecumenical coalition to discuss national problems.

The Catholic church has been the main institutional supporter of the national dialogue sponsored by the National Reconciliation Commission. Indicative of its more activist role, the Catholic church also threw its support behind the ecumenical National Campaign for Life and Peace.

The opposing trends within the church — particularly the split between the spiritualist or sacramentalist elements and those who espouse the theology of liberation — have contributed to the weakness of the institution. Confusion over direction has prompted many to leave the church, with some former Catholics now joining evangelical churches.[36]

The Rise of the Evangelicals

Historically, protestantism and evangelicalism have had a stronger base in Guatemala than in other Central American countries. On a visit to New York City over a hundred years ago, President Barrios requested that the Presbyterian Mission Board dispatch missionaries to Guatemala. In 1882 Presbyterian missionary John Clark Hill arrived in Guatemala City and founded the first Protestant church, which now stands in the shadow of the National Palace. In the 1890s more U.S. Protestant missionaries began arriving in Guatemala aboard U.S. banana boats.

In 1935 the Presbyterian church took the lead in establishing a geographical operating agreement among the traditional evangelical churches in Guatemala. The five main Protestant denominations agreed to divide the country into five regions. The departments of El Progreso, a part of Zacapa, Suchitepéquez, Retalhuleu, and Quezaltenango to the Presbyterians; Quiché and Totonicapán to the Primitive Methodists; Escuintla, Santa Rosa, Jutiapa, Huehuetenango, Sacatepéquez, Jalapa, San Marcos, and Sololá to the Central American Mission; a part of Zacapa, Izabal, and Chiquimula to the Quakers; and Petén, Alta Verapaz, and

Baja Verapaz to the Nazarenes. The Presbyterians and Central American Mission were to share the department of Guatemala. The main reason for the operating agreement among the five traditional denominations was protection against the incursions of new pentecostal churches, notably the Church of God and the Assemblies of God. The older churches were also interested in finding better ways to coordinate their own evangelization.

In these early years, many of the new evangelical missionaries established missions in isolated rural regions. In sharp contrast to the Catholic church, evangelical churches often recognized the need to preach in the numerous native languages of Guatemala and to provide translations of the New Testament. This translation work was greatly expanded in the 1950s when Wycliffe Bible Translators began sending missionaries to the country.

Evangelical churches gradually whittled away at the traditional hold of the Catholic church on the Guatemalan population. But it was not until the 1976 earthquake that the impact of evangelical churches really made its presence felt in Guatemalan society. Along with many other non-governmental organizations, U.S. evangelical missionaries poured into Guatemala after the earthquake. For some, humanitarianism was the main motive for coming. For others, the upheaval caused by the earthquake offered a good opportunity for evangelism. And to some degree, the new evangelical missionaries in the late 1970s were a reflection of the evangelical fervor taking hold in the United States.

Since the mid-1970s the evangelical faiths have been increasing at an unprecedented rate—about 12 percent a year—and show no signs of abating. According to a July 1987 survey by SEPAL, approximately 31.6 percent of the Guatemalan population is evangelical. Within the country there are 9,298 evangelical churches, which works out to almost one church for every 906 Guatemalans. Even the Catholic church now acknowledges that a third of the population is evangelical.[37]

March 23, 1982 is an historic date for evangelicalism in Guatemala. On that date, retired General Efraín Ríos Montt became president of the country in a military coup. Many Guatemalan evangelicals call the coup d'état a miracle or evidence of divine intervention in human affairs. Ríos Montt, who had been a presidential candidate for the Christian Democrats in 1974, was a born-again Christian associated with a California evangelical organization called Gospel Outreach and known as "El Verbo" in Central America. Evangelicals from the United States hailed the fact that Guatemala had a Christian president and proceeded to organize material support for the government and to send hundreds of mission teams to the country. A White House initiative encouraged such groups as Campus Crusade for Christ, Moral Majority, 700 Club, and Youth with a Mission to support the new regime.[38]

The sudden infusion of funds and personnel for U.S. evangelical organizations, plus the free publicity provided by the Guatemalan president's public airing of his religious views, contributed to noticeable growth in the evangelical churches during the Ríos Montt regime. In the Indian highlands, evangelical growth was also a direct result of the army's ongoing counterinsurgency campaign. Since the late 1970s Catholic lay agents and clergy had been subject to escalating repression. Families and sometimes entire communities began attending evangelical services to protect themselves against the accusation of being sympathetic to "radical" elements in the Catholic church. Despite the ouster of Ríos Montt in 1983 and the winding down of the army's war against leftist subversion, evangelical churches are still growing at a brisk rate.

Many evangelical churches banded together in a national campaign, dubbed Plan '90, with two ambitious goals: to make Guatemala 50 percent evangelical by the end of 1990, and to establish an evangelical church for every community of 500 to 1,000 people. This major proselytizing effort was financed and guided by an interdenominational evangelical organization from California named OC Ministries. As elsewhere in Central America, most evangelical denominations and sects are linked to churches in the United States. But there do exist in Guatemala a few impressive local Christian churches, namely the Prince of Peace, Elim, and Shaddai. Although foreign in origin, the historical Protestant churches became national churches in the late 1950s.

Evangelical churches have always had a social-assistance component to their mission in Guatemala. The first modern hospital was established by the Presbyterians. Evangelicals set up numerous primary and secondary schools and even a university. Since the 1976 earthquake the social-service programs of evangelical churches have further expanded. Many churches now have at least minimal daycare, education, health care, or feeding programs associated with their pastoral work. With a few exceptions, most social-assistance programs of the evangelical churches are characterized by their paternalistic nature—mostly handouts accompanied by a Bible message. Virtually all the resources for these programs come from U.S. private agencies, including AMG International, CARE, 700 Club, and World Vision. To a remarkable degree, evangelical pastors credit feeding and schooling programs as a way to spread their religious beliefs. Many say that attention to the children is a way to attract parents to their churches.

GUATEMALA: A COUNTRY GUIDE

GUATEMALA: A COUNTRY GUIDE

As with other Central American countries, the evangelical community in Guatemala is not monolithic. It is divided into a seemingly infinite number of denominations, sects, interdenominational churches and organizations, and alliances. The emphasis of most evangelicals, especially the pentecostal groups, is on individual salvation. The individualism that distinguishes the evangelical community gives rise to a myriad of divisions and tendencies.

Currently, the dominant force is the pentecostal or charismatic sector of evangelicalism, with close links to the Christian right in the United States. New, largely urban denominations like Christian Fraternity, El Verbo, Elim, and Living Water Teaching comprise part of this powerful, highly conservative faction of evangelicalism. Reinforcing this trend are transnational evangelical organizations from the United States like Campus Crusade for Christ, Full Gospel Businessmen's Fellowship International, OC Ministries, and Youth with a Mission. An array of independent U.S. missionaries also bolster this sector of evangelicalism in Guatemala. With narrow theological training and generally no experience in third world countries, individual evangelicals, committed to the Great Commission of evangelism, arrive in Guatemala with Spanish-language Scripture tracts, food and clothing handouts, and the backing of their local church.

The neopentecostal churches and ministries are the most obvious and vocal in the evangelical community, owing to their presence in urban areas and their largely professional and middle-class congregations. Most of these are nondenominational and identify themselves not as "evangelical" but as "Christian" churches, thereby increasing their access to Catholics and former Catholics. But it is the older, mostly fundamentalist churches, like the Assemblies of God, Central American Mission, Church of God, Nazarenes, Baptists, and Presbyterians, that constitute the backbone of the evangelical church in Guatemala. These denominations reach into the most isolated rural areas. The message of personal salvation of the evangelical churches and their often apocalyptic vision have found a niche in communities beset with poverty and wracked by violence. Their strong defense of the family and attacks on drunkenness and other vices have also endeared them to rural communities. The emotional support provided to members by the church community plus the entertainment value generated by almost nightly activities also attract adherents.

Although the evangelical movement is largely conservative, some small and relatively isolated sectors, mainly associated with traditional denominations, have adopted the social interpretations of the theology of liberation. Others are already in the process of breaking with the paternalistic style of social work and encouraging development projects with a more self-determined and less dependent style. Significantly, several church-based social programs have formed an umbrella group to coordinate and further promote development projects by evangelical churches.

In early 1989 Archbishop Penados del Barrio issued a pastoral letter that launched a frontal attack on the evangelicals. Associating evangelical growth with U.S. government aid, the archbishop also charged that the evangelical churches were undermining "the deeply communitarian feeling that exists in the Guatemalan people." In contrast, the pastoral asserted, the Catholic church is the "only element that has managed to establish, between the diverse races and social and economic groups, a certain type of integration." While recent social criticism by the church falls more in the ethos of Vatican II and the Medellín Bishops Conference, the Guatemalan church's pronounced sectarianism does not. Commenting on the pastoral, one evangelical Indian minister, Vitalino Similox, labeled the letter "unfortunate," parrying, "We need to talk of agreements, not differences."[39]

Nongovernmental Organizations

Nongovernmental organizations (NGOs), mainly from the United States, serve as a "privately" sponsored social infrastructure in this country where government services are so notoriously lacking. Guatemala hosts more foreign NGOs than any other Central American country. Among the first foreign NGOs to come to Guatemala were AID-financed groups like CARE, Project Hope, Pan American Development Foundation, and Partners for the Americas, which came to the country as part of the Alliance for Progress in the 1960s. At the same time AID funded local NGOs involved in community and economic development, including Social and Economic Development Institute of Central America (IDESAC), Training Center for Social Promoters (CAPS), and the Cooperative School (EACA).[40]

The disastrous 1976 earthquake, which wracked the highlands, sparked an NGO boom. Scores of NGOs streamed into the devastated area, with most of them staying once the immediate reconstruction and relief work ended. The subsequent scourge of counterinsurgency violence forced many groups out of the highlands, but there has been a new surge in NGO activity in the highlands since 1985.[41]

The Role of AID

The U.S. Agency for International Development (AID) has, since the 1960s, played a critical role in NGO operations and development in Guatemala. It funds NGOs via four avenues: 1) direct funding of U.S. NGOs from the AID/Washington, 2) direct funding of both U.S. and local NGOs from the local AID Mission, 3) indirect funding of both U.S. and local NGOs with local currency funds generated by AID grants, and 4) indirect funding of local NGOs from U.S. NGOs sponsored by AID.

Through its numerous development programs, AID sought to build free-enterprise institutions, foster capitalist growth, obstruct leftist revolution, and promote U.S. trade and investment. Washington can point to successes in all those areas. By promoting rural cooperatives of small farmers, however, AID also unintentionally contributed to the surge of popular organizing in the 1960s and 1970s.

Many rural Guatemalans, particularly the landless and peasant farmers, discovered the limits of AID-style development. Colonizing projects supported by AID often failed because of exploitation of the frontier settlers by wealthy ranchers and investors, army repression, or lack of firm government support. The imported chemical fertilizers and pesticides, which at first seemed like miracles to many campesinos, were later regarded as a new threat to their subsistence as prices climbed and yields fell after several years of intensive chemical usage.

Enthusiasm for AID-sponsored cooperative-formation projects diminished as it became clear that the cooperative federations supported by AID were often controlled from the top by the government and were oriented toward commercial-level farmers. It seemed to many poor Guatemalans that the main benefits of AID's development projects accrued to the elites, both at the national and local levels. The two major problems facing campesinos—lack of land and low wages for farm labor—were not addressed by either AID or the cooperative movement. Having experienced the limitations of government and church-sponsored programs, many peasants joined militant peasant leagues or became guerrilla sympathizers. In the late 1970s and early 1980s NGOs began leaving the highlands and, in some cases, the country. Expatriate NGO staff feared both for their own lives and those of their Guatemalan promoters.

AID in the Eighties

Following a stagnant period during the Lucas García regime, economic aid from the United States has steadily increased. In 1982 AID distributed only $15.5 million in total economic aid, but by 1989 over $147 million in aid dollars were flowing into the country. Guatemala has experienced a similar increase in U.S. food aid, which swelled from $5.6 million in 1982 to $29.7 million in 1989. A substantial part of this new aid has been channeled into NGO programs. This trend began in 1983 when the U.S. Congress prohibited AID from granting new aid to the military government. To keep economic aid flowing into Guatemala, AID distributed funds to NGOs through the National Reconstruction Committee (CRN) and other intermediaries. With government approval, AID has directed most of its development and relief money into the conflictive highlands.

The new emphasis of AID on the highlands coincides with the military's own counterinsurgency priorities. While the military sees development and social-service programs in the highlands in terms of its pacification strategy, AID supports a variety of projects—food-for-work to agricultural production—as part of its economic development strategy and regards NGOs and churches as perfect implementing agents. According to AID documents, NGO programs serve to decrease social discontent, increase economic progress, and raise the level of understanding of the democratic process.

The election of a civilian government in 1986 resulted in a return of many NGOs to the conflictive zones with renewed enthusiasm for once again committing resources to the alleviation of human suffering and to the development of the country. The Christian Democratic government encouraged increased NGO activity, but it did little itself to increase social services or to involve the poor in the development process.

In recent years, AID and U.S. Information Agency (USIA) dollars have been instrumental in the formation and expansion of numerous private-sector lobbying groups, think tanks, and business associations in Guatemala. The stated purpose of this aid is to foster the "growth of democratic institutions" but many feel that the assistance is going only to elite groups and those that support U.S. foreign policy in the region.

AID has attempted to establish the Association of Development and Services Entities of Guatemala (ASINDES) as an NGO umbrella group. But not all has gone according to plan. Many of the original members of ASINDES, which was formed before AID became involved, have left the organization because of AID's domination. Larger U.S. NGOs like CARE have declined to join ASINDES, despite repeated requests by AID, because they prefer to maintain direct funding relations with AID.

In the past, members of ASINDES have expressed concern over Guatemalan government plans to exert increased control over the umbrella group. A 1989 AID regulation granted recipient governments more control over local currency funds (generated by the sale of ESF dol-

lars and Title I food), and many felt that the government would use its en-
hanced role (mainly in bookkeeping and accounting) to favor some
NGOs, especially those that were linked to the Christian Democrats. By
the end of the Cerezo administration, ASINDES was complaining that
AID funds scheduled for ASINDES were being absorbed by the government.

AID funds for private organizations go overwhelmingly to business associations and promotional groups — not to those involved in providing
community services. As such, many millions of dollars are flowing to
private-sector groups that represent the economic elite of the society.
These AID-funded business organizations generally exert a reactionary
presence, being strongly opposed to government plans to increase taxes,
redistribute land, and meet the wage and social demands of popular organizations and unions.

NGOs and Counterinsurgency

Private groups, both local and foreign, have often served the interests
of the military's counterinsurgency campaign. A nexus for NGO-govern-
ment-military cooperation in rural pacification is the National
Reconstruction Committee (CRN). Together with the closely associated
Army Civil Affairs division, the CRN coordinates NGO activity in most
conflictive areas. AID has channeled local currency funds to CRN-coor-
dinated NGO projects involving such groups as World Vision, Project
Hope, Food for the Hungry, and the archdiocesan CARITAS.[42] As part
of its coordinating role, the CRN has also attempted to serve as a registry
and clearinghouse for NGOs in Guatemala, although numerous NGOs
have simply refused to cooperate.

A small number of NGOs work directly with the military in pacification programs. These include such rightwing groups as the Air Commando Association, Knights of Malta, Food for the Hungry, Americans for a
Free Central America, Carroll Behrhorst Development Foundation,
PAVA, and the National Defense Foundation, in addition to numerous
evangelical groups like Youth with a Mission and the Summer Institute
of Linguistics. The Air Commando Association, for example, works
directly under military supervision in the Quiché area providing medical
services, and Food for the Hungry collaborates with Army Civil Affairs
in facilitating relocation of displaced Indians into model villages. Also integrated into the military's game plan are several U.S. NGOs, like Friends
of the Americas and CAUSA, who make no secret of their rightwing
ideology.

In carrying out the "development" aspect of its National Development and Security Plan, the military can also count on numerous local NGOs who share the army's counterinsurgency perspective. These include such private-sector groups as COPRONIHUAC (founded by a director of *La Prensa Libre*) and the archdiocesan CARITAS, which distributes food and other supplies to displaced people living under military control.

There are many other NGOs whose humanitarian and development work has little if anything to do with counterinsurgency operations. But even much of this NGO activity does have political implications. The CARE and SHARE food-for-work projects in Guatemala City were explicitly designed to forestall urban unrest that might be unleashed as a result of the Cerezo government's economic-stabilization plans, for example.

Heather Nesbitt, a CARE official in Guatemala, said she believes that "an agency like CARE can maintain its integrity and even moderate the army's approach to meeting people's needs, while small aid groups can only carry out band-aid work and may be vulnerable to military pressure."[43] In 1987, Nesbitt was among 90 NGO workers who received a gold medal from the Ministry of Defense. Major Luis Siekavizza of the army's Civil Affairs division offered that the army prefers to work with large international NGOs rather than with small groups "that do not understand the three basics of development in Guatemala: health, education, and security." It was also his opinion that when "peasants here see them [international NGOs] working with us, they understand that the army has international support."[44]

Most NGO activity in Guatemala is characterized by its paternalistic, welfare nature, in contrast to a style of NGO assistance more supportive of community organizing and popular education. Several NGOs do attempt to explore the limits imposed by repression by sponsoring such projects, but on the whole NGO work in Guatemala has a charitable character that serves to pacify people and attempts to mollify the social costs of counterinsurgency. The most progressive NGO activity is sponsored by European and Canadian agencies and, to a lesser extent, by progressive Protestant churches and Catholic orders in the United States.[45]

Women and Feminism

The women's movement in Guatemala is the least developed in Central America, both in terms of organizing at the popular level and among educated women. This is largely attributable to the high level of repression that has beset the country for over 35 years. The highly divided nature of Guatemalan society—both in class and race—and the low level of schooling are other factors.

It was during the 1944-1954 period that Guatemalan women first began organizing. The Guatemalan Women's Alliance, an organization of teachers and other working women, began during those years. In 1945, women obtained the right to vote. The military coup of 1954 brought to a violent conclusion this decade of democracy and halted the advance of women's organizing. In the late 1960s, another women's group formed and was named after Dolores Bedoya, a heroine of the country's independence movement. This new group, however, was an association of professionals and upper-class women who had no connection to the popular sectors.

In 1975, at the beginning of a new stage of popular organizing, the Women's Solidarity in Action committee flowered briefly. Another short-lived attempt to organize women was the National Women's Union (UNAMG), which disbanded shortly after its founding in 1980 due to the intensifying violence of the Lucas García regime. Other women's organizations did exist but were mostly associations of upper-class women who met for charitable or professional purposes rather than to organize for social change.

The advent of the Cerezo government opened up political space for serious popular organizing, and women took advantage of this opportunity to form human rights organizations and groups concerned specifically with the situation of women. In addition, the new administration's placement of women in high government positions played a role in increasing feminist consciousness in Guatemala. The Mutual Support Group (GAM), a human rights organization directed principally by women, has succeeded in focusing international concern over continued human rights violations and the plight of widows.

In 1988 GAM was joined by another women's human rights organization called the National Coordinator of Guatemalan Widows (CONAVIGUA), whose directors and members are mostly Indian widows of the murdered and disappeared. According to Rigoberta Menchú, an opposition representative, CONAVIGUA is "the first organization in all the 500 years of Guatemala that was born of indigenous women. It is an organization so powerful that the indigenous women can channel the convictions of thousands of other Guatemalan women."

Another significant step forward for the women's movement in the 1980s was the creation in 1986 of the GRUFEPROMEFAM, a women's organization linked to the UNSITRAGUA union confederation. At first, it was simply an auxiliary organization to raise political consciousness among the wives of union activists, but GRUFEPROMEFAM quickly expanded to include union women and later women from all popular sectors. Its agenda is closely linked to the popular movement, but it also has a distinct focus on gender issues, one of which is to formulate a history of women's organizing in Guatemala. The success of the First Conference of Guatemalan Women Workers, which GRUFEPROMEFAM sponsored in 1989, encouraged the organization to make more ties with the popular movement and to strengthen its links with the women's movement in other Central American countries. Its slogan is: "Together always for the unity of our families and for a better society." Another new organization is the Coordinator of Guatemalan Women's Groups (COAMUGUA), which, in addition to coordinating various women's projects, is attempting to organize national forums about women's issues.

Living conditions for Guatemalan women are among the worst in the hemisphere. Poor women, particularly Indian women, are treated as slaves, especially the ones who work for as little as $40 a month as maids. Some 47 percent of Guatemalan men are literate, but only 37 percent of women know how to read and write — a percentage that drops to 25 percent for Indian women. During the 1980s, many women sought outside income (rising from 13 to 24 percent of the official workforce since 1981), most of them working as street vendors in urban areas. The majority of the country's refugees and internally displaced are women.[46]

Native People

The Indian people of Guatemala are not a minority. They are a majority, but one which has been resolutely excluded from the national power structure. Estimates of native people in Guatemala range from 38 percent (government statistics) to 70 percent, but most sources indicate that Indians constitute at least half of Guatemalan society.

The Indians of Guatemala are descendants of the Mayan Indian civilization. They are, however, divided into 21 different language groups (principally Quichi, Cakchiquel, Kekcha, and Mam). When the Spanish arrived in Guatemala, the major Indian groups were locked in bitter rivalry, facilitating their colonization. There was, however, no one decisive conquest because there was no single Indian civilization to subdue. Estimates range as high as 90 percent when gauging the precipitous drop in the Mesoamerican Indian population during the first century of conquest, due mainly to the spread of disease.

Today, although the numerical majority, Guatemalan Indians are relegated to the margins of society. Isolated in terms of language and politics, their exploitation is a cornerstone of the national economy. Guatemala's agroexport system has been built on the backs of cheap Indian labor. Tourism, the country's second largest source of foreign exchange, is also largely dependent on the native community.[47]

For five hundred tortuous years since colonization, the Indians of Guatemala have endured, retaining much of their culture and community. This determination to survive as a cultural and ethnic group has not meant that the Indian people have resisted the advances of the modern world, as many might assume. Indian farmers, for example, have readily recognized the value of new agricultural practices and the potential of marketing cooperatives.

Continued cultural survival in Guatemala is being increasingly undermined — the main threat being the ongoing counterinsurgency war which since the mid-1970s has included a strategy of ethnocide. In 1984 the World Council of Indigenous Peoples accused the military of pursuing a "policy of systematic extermination of the Indian population of Guatemala." In response to these accusations of ethnocide, the military claims that it focuses its counterinsurgency campaign in the highlands only because that is the stronghold of guerrilla support. Critics, however, charge that only the racism of Guatemalan society can explain the wholesale horror of the war that has eliminated over 400 Indian villages.[48]

Massacres of Indian communities thought to be sympathetic to leftist guerrillas (themselves largely Indian) is only one element of this ethnocide. As part of its pacification plan, the army has attempted to restructure and reprogram Indian communities. Development poles, model villages, strategic re-education camps, penetration roads, obligatory civil patrols, and the encouragement of evangelical proselytizing are all part of the army's overall plan to undermine Indian community and to assert the dominance of "the national identity." As a psychological action plan for the Ixil Triangle described it, the purpose of pacification is "to capture the mentality of the Ixils to make them feel part of the Guatemalan nation."[49]

Cultural survival is also a matter of economic survival. Without agrarian reform, there is no longer enough land to support the Indian population, which continues to grow despite the persecution. The lack of land is forcing entire Indian families to relocate to the urban slums, initiating the all but inevitable loss of cultural identity. Large sectors of Indian society are living in a state of shock brought on by the economic and political crisis. They have been displaced from their homes, have lost their families, and are being subjected to a systematic military campaign of psychological operations.

Indians and the Popular Movement

In the late 1970s the army suddenly realized that the Indians of the highlands were quickly becoming an insurgent population. The socioeconomic conditions—particularly the land crisis—certainly provided cause for rebellion. But it was a combination of the new social teachings of the church, the focus on cooperative formation by many foreign development groups, and the popular education programs of the guerrillas that sparked what the army considered to be a widespread Indian revolt. What was so threatening, from the army's point of view, was the way whole communities suddenly seemed to adopt an organized posture in the face of deteriorating socioeconomic conditions.

The terror unleashed by the military was designed to undercut this wave of popular organizing and to force the Indian population to submit to military control. In the process, hundreds of villages were razed, tens of thousands killed, and hundreds of thousands displaced.

The army's Security and Development strategy for the highlands brought popular organizing, except for the guerrillas forces, to a halt. But in the later part of the 1980s, independent popular organizations once again began to emerge among Indian communities. Most of the members of the GAM human rights group are Indian women, and the same is true for CONAVIGUA, which was founded by Indian widows in 1988. Among its objectives are fighting against the "abuse, rape, and exploitation which we suffer at the hands of soldiers, civil patrol leaders, and military commissioners," and helping Guatemalan women, particularly rural Indian women "become conscious and active in the struggle for the well-being of the community."

Another Indian-based group is the Runajel Junam Council of Ethnic Communities (CERJ), also founded in 1988. The first activity by this Quiché group was a march in Guatemala City denouncing civil patrol abuses. Its director, Amilcar Méndez, is *ladino* but its membership is virtually all Indian. The Campesino Unity Committee (CUC), an Indian-led organization of peasants forced underground during the scourge of blood-shedding in the early 1980s, resumed organizing in 1988. CUC explains it is fighting "to have one more *tortilla* for our children." Like the other Indian organizations, CUC is more than a protest organization. It has a positive program for economic and social justice. Another Indian organization is the Highland Campesino Committee (CCDA), which was founded in 1982 and works mainly in Sololá and Chimaltenango.

The Fourth World

Nationalism has been a political current among certain sectors of the Indian population since the mid-1960s. This current reemerged in the middle of the 1980s, especially among some middle-class and professional Indians. To some degree, this resurfacing of Indian nationalism has been a product of the disillusion, deception, and betrayal that many Guatemalan Indians felt after the ethnocidal counterinsurgency campaigns of the early 1980s. In large part, this feeling of betrayal by the guerrillas was fostered by the military in its attempt to lay full blame for the violence on the guerrillas. At the same time, though, many Indians felt they had been used as pawns and sacrificial lambs by the *ladino* guerrilla leadership.

One current of Indian nationalism is known as the "Fourth World" theory. Basically, Fourth World adherents believe that Indians have little in common with *ladinos*, even poor ones. Indians are thought to be inherently different from non-Indians, who, coming from a Western industrialized culture, will never understand or respect Indian lives and culture. Indians in Guatemala live in a Fourth World.[50] They are "caught in the middle, and are being moved around like pawns on a chessboard."[51]

This and other currents of nationalism have been echoed and promoted by such U.S. groups as Akwesasne Notes, National Indian Youth Council, and the Indian Law Resource Center. Many Indian groups which supported anti-Sandinista Miskito Indians like Brooklyn Rivera and Steadman Fagoth also support an "Indian alternative" for Guatemala. Other Indian groups, like the International Indian Treaty Council, have denounced this separatist view as being counterrevolutionary and an instrument of U.S. foreign policy.

Within Guatemala Indian nationalism finds resonance and definition in the teachings and writings of the controversial anthropologist Carlos Guzmán Bockler, who in various books encourages the revival of a Mesoamerican Indian nation. Guzmán argues that Indian problems are race-rooted rather than of a class nature. He feels that an "Indian war" may be necessary to protect Indian rights and assert Indian culture. Like the Fourth World advocates, Guzmán feels that Western culture and civilization have been forcibly imposed on Indian communities and need to be discarded. Guzmán, like other advocates of Indian nationalism, lumps leftist guerrillas with other racist "Westerners."[52]

In contrast to the Fourth World response to this type of cultural-nationalist analysis, Ja C'amabal I'b, a collective of Guatemalan Indians living in Mexico, proclaims:

We are opposed to those theories which, through a desire, whether sincere or not, of preserving what is Indian from all "contamination of the West," in reality imply renouncement of the knowledge that we need to make our struggle for liberation effective. This would condemn our struggle to romanticism and failure.[53]

Revolutionary Movement: The Indigenous Question

The leftist revolutionary movement has struggled with questions about ethnicity and revolution since the early 1960s. At first, questions about Indian issues and the role of indigenous people in the revolution were interpreted solely in terms of the Marxist doctrines of the Guatemalan Communist Party (PGT) and the country's first guerrilla front, Rebel Armed Forces (FAR). Indians were considered to be unorganizable and too passive to take an active role in revolutionary struggle. This reasoning partly explains the decision to focus the first guerrilla *"foco"* in an area of northeastern Guatemala populated mostly by *ladino* peasants.

It was not until the late 1960s that Guatemalan insurgents recognized the revolutionary potential of the Indian majority. When the guerrilla forces resurfaced in the late 1970s, the focus of their organizing was on the Indian communities of the *altiplano*. The three major organizations— Guerrilla Army of the Poor (EGP), which targeted northern Huehuetenango and Quiché; Revolutionary Organization of People in Arms (ORPA), which organized in Sololá and San Marcos; and FAR, which established its base in the Petén—took more care this time in promoting Indian leadership and presenting the revolutionary struggle in terms of Indian interests.

While more conscious of racism and the need to integrate Indians into the struggle, the guerrilla leadership has not, however, fully developed an analysis of ethnic issues. Guatemalan National Revolutionary Unity (URNG), the guerrilla coalition, currently places high priority on what it calls "ethnic-national questions," while cautioning against the dangers of Indian nationalism. URNG defines the revolution as a war on two fronts: "The situation of the Indian as both oppressed and exploited, in which class contradictions are linked to ethnic-national contradictions is what gives the Guatemalan revolution its special character." Further clarifying this commitment to resolving ethnic-national questions, URNG declared:

The revolutionary movement must respect, with great dedication, the legitimate rights of the ethnic-national groups, creating economic and political bases which will allow them real access to the entire society. The participation at the directorate and every level of the guerrilla movement, as well as full participation at the national level after we take power, is the prerequisite for all possible change.

Both from within and outside the guerrilla forces, Guatemalan Indians themselves, like Rigoberta Menchú, are also trying to determine the extent and nature of ethnic-national questions in Guatemala. As Domingo Hernández, a member of Ja C'amabal I'b, reflected: "[We] Indians are just now beginning to analyze for ourselves our vision for the society to which we belong, what we think of the new society, what we think of our own culture and identity, of our particular needs and desires."

Despite the advances made by URNG leaders, many Indians feel that the guerrilla leadership still clings to old models. As one critique proposed: "The revolution must be a political method, through which the popular masses decide their destiny, not an already decided system. The Indian must play a protagonist role, a role not won as a concession, but rightfully owned."[54] In addition to the new positions on the indigenous question being developed within URNG, other positions are being put forth by leftist groups like PGT-6th of January and Revolutionary October which insist on local regional autonomy for Indian communities within a revolutionary state, a position also held by some Indian revolutionary organizations.

Refugees and the Internally Displaced

The military coup of 1954 marked the beginning of the diaspora of Guatemalans. (The term "refugees" refers to those persons who have fled their country of origin and take refuge in another country, while "displaced" refers to those who have been forced to leave their home but still live within the country.) Until 1980 most of those fleeing the country were *ladino* activists and politicians. The 1980s, however, was the decade of mass Indian emigration. A people who for so long have clutched tenaciously to their land fled on foot before the advancing terror that swept across the highlands. Political violence has forced an estimated 500,000 to one million Guatemalans to abandon their homes in the last ten years.[55]

Most of those fleeing the country head north to Mexico, with many persevering to the United States or Canada. One measure of this refugee population is the number of Guatemalans living under United Nations' protection. In Mexico, some 40,000 Guatemalans inhabit UN-sponsored camps, while in Belize there are 1200 with another 380 in Honduras and 400 in Nicaragua. But the majority of those who have fled Guatemala are not tabulated as official refugees. Instead, they live and work in the shadows as undocumented residents, mainly in Mexico and the United States.

Guatemalans in the United States

Guatemalans who find their way to the United States enter not as refugees but as illegal aliens. Over the last ten years, an estimated 50,000 to 200,000 Guatemalans have entered the United States. To get to the United States, these illegal immigrants suffer graft, robbery, rape, and imprisonment in Mexico. Sexual abuse of Central American women passing through Mexico is thought to be as high as 50 percent.[56] The greatest concentration of Guatemalans is in Los Angeles, with other large communities in Houston, Washington, New York City, Chicago, and San Francisco. In the eyes of the U.S. government, however, these Guatemalan exiles in the United States are not political refugees deserving of special care and protection but simply economic immigrants seeking a better life.

Despite tighter border patrols, the Immigration and Naturalization Service (INS) reports that Guatemalans continue to enter the country in large numbers. In 1988, the number of Guatemalans apprehended by the INS increased by 38 percent. A new INS tactic is to attempt to stop the flow "in the pipeline," meaning discouraging immigrants from ever reaching the United States. It has launched a "public awareness blitz" in Guatemala and other Central American countries in an attempt to slow the northward migration. As part of a monitoring project, the U.S. government assigned two intelligence officers, two Border Patrol officials, an Immigration Officer, and two Anti-Smuggling agents to Guatemala. Among other things, the agents were to "gather predictive intelligence...working with law enforcement officials at those sites."[57]

While the U.S. government is trying to find ways to stem the tide of Guatemalans, human rights groups like Amnesty International and many U.S. church organizations call upon the government to grant them refugee status. In 1988, asylum applications from Guatemalans rose nearly 900 percent from the previous year. Yet INS granted asylum status to only 5 percent of the Guatemalans who applied, compared to 53 percent of Nicaraguans.[58]

Repatriation and Resettlement

In the early 1980s the military lashed out at reports that tens of thousands of Indians were seeking refuge outside the country, charging that the reports were part of an international communist conspiracy to discredit Guatemala. For years, the military regime did not acknowledge the existence of a large refugee population—much as the Honduras government denied that the contras had made their base inside Honduras. Yet while the military government was dismissing reports of an increasing refugee population in Mexico, its troops knew better, crossing the border repeatedly to terrorize the refugees.

Inside Guatemala, the army readily acknowledged the growing displaced population, but alleged these victims were all fleeing from the guerrillas. Corralled in model villages and internment camps controlled by the army's civil affairs (S-5) specialists, the displaced Indians themselves often corroborated the army's version of events. In Mexico, however, the refugee population was less intimidated and offered a decidedly different version of what had caused them to flee the country.

The continued existence of large numbers of refugees in Mexico has proved embarrassing to the army and the government. The refugees are clear testimony to the savagery of the country's armed forces, and their fear of returning home indicate that conditions have not substantially improved under the civilian government. To rectify this embarrassment, the Cerezo government in 1986 created the CEAR (Special Commission to Aid Repatriates) as a government agency to work with the United Nations to facilitate the repatriation of refugees. Two years later the name changed to CEARD, adding the "D" to reflect the commission's work with the internally displaced.

CEARD has had limited success in persuading Guatemalans to come home. By early 1990 only some 4300 refugees had repatriated under joint CEARD-UN sponsorship. Each year CEARD claims that there will be an influx of repatriates but continued fear keeps most refugees from leaving the camps in Mexico. The experience of many of those who have returned reaffirms their distrust of the Guatemalan government. Contrary to government promises, there have been numerous cases of returning refugees being subjected to army interrogation and detention. The Guatemala refugees in Mexico have established a communications and organizing network and have presented demands to the National Reconciliation Commission (CNR).

Refugees have arrived in their home village only to find their land has been confiscated for model villages or redistributed by INTA (Institute for Agrarian Transformation) to other peasants considered more loyal to the army. Some have been tortured and killed, and returning refugees are often conscripted into civil patrols. Responding to government initiatives, the refugee community in Mexico has said that it will not return until certain conditions are met: return is strictly voluntary, all land belonging to refugees is returned, the right to organize and freely associate is honored, and the right to personal safety and security is assured.

Increasingly, CEARD's work has been with displaced persons, most of whom have been driven from mountain hideouts by army offensives. In 1988 CEARD assisted and helped resettle most of the 4,500 displaced Guatemalans rounded up by the military in sweeps through the northern highlands. Unable to weed out the guerrillas, army counterinsurgency units have focused attention on the displaced, mostly in the Ixil Triangle area. Once out of the mountains and in army hands, these displaced Indians are subjected to an army psychological operations campaign that includes "civic and democratic education," housing in resettlement villages, and the distribution of food and medical services.

Displaced Guatemalans have also formed their own organizations. Those still living outside areas of military control have organized the Communities of Population in Resistance (CPR).[59] In the northern highlands and in the Petén there are numerous communities of displaced families and returning refugees who have chosen to live clandestinely in the mountains and jungles rather than to resubmit to military control. These communities, which have been remarkably successful in creating new cooperative structures and self-sufficient economies, are part of the new popular base of the guerrilla movement. The CPR communities say that they are fighting to protect their inalienable right to internal refuge so they can "survive, maintain our cultures, and defend our rights as Guatemalans."[60] Other displaced Guatemalans organized the National Council of the Displaced (CONDEG) to protect their interests and rights in the face of continuing military repression.

Economic and military disruption have left 3.8 million Guatemalans living without adequate shelter. Archbishop Penados del Barrio has noted that "almost 50 percent of Guatemalans live in something that cannot be called a house. These inhumane conditions are a symptom of an unjust social, political, and economic system imposed on the majority and maintained by force."[61]

Nature and Environmentalism

The quetzal, the fabulously plumaged bird few have ever seen, is the national bird of Guatemala. It has given its name to the national currency and the country's second largest city. The quetzal is the symbol of Guatemala.

One of the few places you can hope to see a quetzal is at the Quetzal Reserve on the road to Cobán in Alta Verapaz. The lush green of the reserve stands in tragic contrast to the deforested country that surrounds the national bird's final sanctuary. It is a creature of the cloud forest — misty jungles of deep-green ferns and impenetrable foliage that once covered the mountains of the Guatemalan highlands. Today, the range of the quetzal is only 2500 kilometers. By the year 2000 the Guatemalan quetzal may be extinct. All that will be left are the few stuffed birds one sees in the National Palace and dusty museums. Images of the fabled bird will remain woven into the *huipiles* and blankets of the native people of this deforested land.

Guatemala is famous for its beauty and environmental wealth. As the northernmost point of the isthmian bridge between the two American continents, the country hosts an extraordinary ecological diversity. Its habitats support 250 species of mammals, 664 of birds, 231 of reptiles, and 220 of freshwater fish. Such food crops as maize, runner beans, tomatoes, and cocoa all originated in the historic Mayan civilizations of Mexico and Guatemala.[62] According to some botanists, Guatemala hosts the richest and most diverse flora in Central America, with some 8,000 species of vascular plants. It is, however, an environment devastated by distorted patterns of land use, a counterinsurgency war, and a search for survival by the peasant population.

The facts of environmental destruction are as horrifying as the data on ecological diversity is impressive. The country is losing its remaining forest cover at the rate of 2.3 percent a year. Some 65 percent of the country's original forest cover has been destroyed, most in the last three decades.

The pine forests found in the central highlands of Guatemala are largely secondary growth which has occurred after the original hardwood trees were cut.[63] The country's rich mangrove forests, potentially a bountiful source of shrimp and fish, are rapidly being raped by reckless development, 40 percent of the mangroves having seriously degenerated since 1965.[64]

An estimated 25 to 35 percent of the land cover is considered eroded or seriously degraded.[65] About two-thirds of the Guatemalan land mass is highly susceptible to soil erosion because so much of the soil is unconsolidated volcanic ash located on fragile slopes. The high population density — 469 persons to each square kilometer of cultivated land — represents a serious threat to soil stability. Annual soil runoff in Guatemala is estimated to vary between 20 and 300 metric tons per hectare in areas still under vegetative cover to between 700 and 1,100 metric tons per hectare in unforested areas.[66]

Extensive soil erosion resulting from deforestation and hillside farming have caused serious silting of rivers and lakes. The carrying capacity of the Motagua River was reduced by 50 percent between 1960 and 1980 by sedimentation, a process causing flooding and threatening irrigation projects. Agricultural development on the steep slopes are contributing to the rapid siltation of Lake Atitlán. Mining and lumber operations are causing serious sedimentation in Lake Izabal.[67]

Hydroelectric power too has brought ecological, financial, and human catastrophe to Guatemala. Financed by the World Bank and the Inter-American Development Bank (IDB), hydroelectric projects like the infamous Chixoy Power Plant have forced thousands of peasant families off their lands, leaving in its wake massive deforestation and evaporative water loss without providing the promised cost-efficient energy. These projects also account for about half the country's external debt.

The most alarming environmental destruction is in the isolated department of Petén, where 20 percent of the forest has been razed in the past decade. At the center of the devastation of this region, considered by many as one of the world's lungs, has been the military-administered Petén Development Board (FYDEP), which has controlled life in this sparsely populated department. Rather than curtailing timbering, FYDEP encouraged it, even to the extent of permitting the Mexican lumber industry to illegally export timber from the Petén. Despite government decrees prohibiting the unregulated cutting of hardwoods, lumber operations like the giant Asseradero del Norte sawmill continue clearing the forests of giant mahogany and cedar.[68]

Another environmental pressure stems from peasant farmers who practice "slash and burn" agriculture, which after several years leaves land suitable only for pasture. Up to 5 million cubic meters of wood, much of it tropical hardwood, are wasted each year in the Petén region as a result of clearing and burning.[69]

Oil exploration and drilling also threatens the Petén, but rising local and international concern about Central American rainforests may result in further protections against the oil industry. Such was the case in mid-1989 when the government, bowing to environmental pressure, announced the suspension of a lease that would have permitted Exxon to drill for oil on the protected archaeological site of El Ceibal. Guerrilla sabotage has also obstructed further petroleum development in Guatemala.

The Ravages of War

War is another enemy of the environment. Scorched-earth tactics and aerial bombing have left scars across the face of the highlands and the Petén. In some areas, so much of the forest has been destroyed by the war that local peasants can no longer find enough wood for cooking and heating. The boom in war-related road building, funded by AID and other foreign donors, represents a serious short-term and long-term threat to the environment in conflictive zones. AID, the World Food Program (which sponsors food-for-work road-building programs), and the government call them farm-to-market routes, but for the army these are often penetration roads that link the most isolated areas to military bases.

In conflictive areas, the army, using local civil patrols as "voluntary" labor, deforested large swaths of forest on both sides of new and existing roads to avoid ambushes. These new travel links tattooing the highlands not only facilitate the counterinsurgency war but also open these areas to new forms of economic exploitation, including clearcutting by the lumber industry. In the Ixcán, the military also controls logging permits, making juicy commissions for deforesting this conflictive region. On a much smaller scale, guerrilla forces also contribute to deforestation, often felling trees to form roadblocks.

A new environmental threat is the U.S.-sponsored "War on Drugs," which involves widespread spraying of vegetated areas with such glycophosphate herbicides as Round-Up. Although Guatemala does not even appear on the UN's list of drug-growing nations, since 1987 the Drug Enforcement Administration (DEA) and the State Department have used DEA planes for extensive aerial spraying of areas of the Petén and the highlands. The spraying, which supposedly targets marijuana and poppy-growing areas, has elicited protests from affected communities who report deaths, illnesses, and non-drug crop losses as a result of the program. In early 1988, the decimation was briefly halted after reports of more than a dozen related deaths in San Marcos and the Petén but spraying soon resumed. Critics in Guatemala claim that in addition to Round-Up, such restricted-use chemicals as paraquat, malathion, and EDB have also been used in the defoliation campaign.

There is a drug business in Guatemala but it is unlikely that this military-controlled industry is the target of the DEA and State Department anti-drug campaign. In isolated rural areas, active and retired military officials reportedly operate drug plantations, while in the cities police are partners in the drug sale business. Guerrillas charge that the army, with DEA financing and cooperation, is actually defoliating those isolated areas suspected of harboring revolutionaries and displaced.

The Plague of Pesticides

Excessive pesticide use renders farm labor on the agroexport plantations dangerous work. Along the littoral highway, that fringing the fertile coastal plain, billboards advertise chemicals which are banned in the United States. The chemical fog that clings to these flatlands leaves your eyes smarting and your lungs gasping for breath. For the farmworkers, the heavy, careless use of agricultural chemicals on the south coast plantations is just another nail in the coffin enveloping their hard and unnaturally short lives. Guatemalans are said to have more DDT in their body fat than any other society.

It used to be that the chemical war against the environment was confined to the hot and humid coast. In the last 20 years, however, chemicals have been integrated into the agricultural practices of small peasant farmers in the *altiplano* as well, thanks to promotion by extension agents and foreign-development agencies. In recent years, chemical use has soared due to programs to promote the production of blemish-free nontraditional agroexports. Even in the United States, the production of spotless produce necessitates frequent sprayings. In tropical climates like that of Guatemala, almost constant pesticide application is needed to grow fruits and vegetables acceptable for the U.S. market. This new focus on nontraditional agroexports has resulted in a rash of health problems and threatens the environmental balance of the *altiplano*. Another sinister problem is that produce rejected by U.S. buyers due to excessive chemical input is sold on the local market to unsuspecting consumers. According to an official at the country's Social Security Institute, "In Guatemala, food can have all the insecticides in the world, and still be sold on the local market."[70]

A related concern is the USDA-sponsored Med-fly control project, which uses the cancer-causing EDB pesticide (banned in the United States since 1984) even though there is no hard evidence that the flies are threatening local crops or are heading north from Guatemala to endanger U.S. crops.

The Urban Nightmare

The environmental destruction triggered by rapid and uncontrolled urbanization has not been quantified or scientifically assessed. But there is little doubt that urbanization, particularly in sprawling Guatemala City, is laying waste to the environment while slowly choking the life out of city residents.

The acrid odor of burning garbage from city dumps, which blankets Guatemala City during the night, is perhaps the most repulsive symptom of this urban nightmare. Every day Guatemala City produces 1400 tons of garbage. Since the city has no facilities to treat this waste, it is simply burnt and used as landfill.

Diesel fumes clog both the city's air and the lungs of its inhabitants. Street vendors report high incidences of lung and heart diseases. So thick are the fumes that the faces of pedestrians are uniformly covered with a thin dark coat of carbon and chemicals.

Environmental Activism

The Cerezo government hopped aboard the environmentalist bandwagon with its creation of the National Commission for the Environment (CONAMA), which was headed by Jorge Cabrera, brother of presidential candidate Alfonso Cabrera. The commission has exhibited measured concern about the continuing destruction of the country's environment, although its initiatives have been largely limited to proposals for wilderness reserves and empty decrees against deforestation. As with other national commissions, CONAMA includes a representative from the Ministry of Defense. In addition to its real concerns about environmental destruction, the Cerezo government sees environmental protection as a source of foreign revenue from international agencies concerned about rainforest destruction.

The government promised to create a Ministry of Natural Resources in 1990, but even if established it would likely suffer the fate of other related government agencies which are underfunded and lack enforcement authority. For example, though lumber export is prohibited, both Guatemalan and Mexican timber companies continue to fell the remaining forest reserve at the annual rate of 153,000 hectares, with much of it destined for foreign markets.

What exists of the environmental movement is limited to small organizations of professionals and students. The main environmental group is Defenders of Nature, which has recommended the creation of private wildlife reserves and has plans for a popular education campaign about resource depletion. One of the country's earliest environmentalists was Mario Dary, who founded the University of San Carlos environmental program that established the Quetzal Reserve. In December 1981, Dary was murdered in Guatemala City. It is commonly speculated in Guatemala that lumber interests, who felt threatened by Dary's efforts to protect the highland forests, may have had a hand in his killing.[71]

Chapter 5

Foreign Influence

U.S Foreign Policy

Between Guatemala and the United States there has existed a long-term sharing of foreign-policy interests. This alliance has been the natural result of the historic predominance of U.S. trade and investment in the Guatemalan economy. Washington's foreign-policy interests in Guatemala also arise from the perceived Monroe Doctrine prerogative to manage the politics of countries considered to be the backyard of the United States and, more specifically, from U.S. concerns that the leftist challenge in Guatemala could spread north to Mexico.

Describing U.S. foreign-policy interests in the region, the U.S. Agency for International Development (AID) in 1989 told Congress, "In terms of U.S. interests in Central America, Guatemala occupies a key position because it has the largest population and strongest economy in the region and has only recently returned to democratic government. The success of democracy and of free-market-based economic reform will have a profound effect on the entire region and act as a brake on Marxist-Leninist expansion."[1]

Relations Sour and Sweeten

Relations were shaken in 1977 by the Carter administration's insistence that Guatemala improve its human rights record. Between 1977 and 1983 government-to-government links between the two nations weakened, obligating Guatemala to seek out aid from other countries including Israel, Taiwan, South Africa, and the military regime in Argentina. Nevertheless, U.S.-Guatemala relations were never completely severed, and small levels of U.S. economic and military aid continued to flow to Guatemala.[2]

Relations began to warm again after President Reagan took office. New commercial arms deliveries were approved by the White House, which also attempted to persuade Congress to increase economic aid and renew direct military aid.[3] As the Guatemalan army began to wind down its campaign of terror and the country moved toward civilian rule, close U.S. ties with Guatemala were renewed. Although Democratic Party critics of Guatemala's human rights practices prevented the Reagan administration from supplying the country with large quantities of direct military aid, U.S. economic assistance steadily increased during the decade and direct military aid was resumed in 1986, although only for nonlethal supplies and training.

Since 1983 the United States has supported a program of political and economic stabilization counterpointing a similar effort sponsored by the Guatemalan military. Among the elements of this assistance are the following:

* Large injections of balance-of-payments economic assistance.

* Development assistance and local currency funding to support the military-controlled pacification campaign in the conflictive areas.

* An economic-growth strategy based on the promotion of private-sector investment, particularly in nontraditional exports.

* Military aid, training, and arms sales to support the army's counterinsurgency efforts and to link it more firmly to the United States.

* Support for the "democratization" process through economic-aid programs that finance the election process, policy think tanks, police training, judicial reform programs, and new business associations.

* Financial and diplomatic backing for generous multilateral aid programs from multilateral financial institutions such as the Interamerican Development Bank and related efforts to improve the international standing of Guatemala.

U.S. Assistance Strategy

U.S. foreign policy towards Guatemala is a variation of its overall Central American policy. Like its neighbors Honduras and El Salvador, Guatemala has been regarded by the U.S. government as a democratic success story. According to Washington, the economic salvation of Guatemala, as with other Central American countries, depends upon efforts by the government and AID to promote private-sector investment and nontraditional exports, uplifting the poor via the magic of the marketplace.

Yet there are some major differences, too. Unlike in El Salvador, where Washington wholeheartedly and unabashedly supports the counterinsurgency war, the U.S. embassy has tried to maintain some public distance between itself and the Guatemalan military. Through the CIA, the Defense Intelligence Agency (DIA), and the U.S. military's liaison office in the country, the U.S. government does maintain a wealth of information not only about the counterinsurgency war but also about the entire system of political surveillance and assassination run by the Guatemalan army.[4]

Direct military aid has been held to a minimum due to persistent congressional and international concerns about the savagery of the Guatemalan security forces. Nonetheless, military aid has steadily increased in the late 1980s and has been supplemented by indirect military aid through civic-action and drug-enforcement programs as well as the unleashing of new commercial military sales. In the 1980s Guatemala received increasing allocations of all forms of U.S. economic aid, ranging from food aid and trade credits to economic support funds and an expanded Peace Corps program.

In its attempts to stabilize the country, the U.S. government has, to a large degree, accepted the limits set by the oligarchy. The same is true with the military, which itself has set the security and development, as well as the democratization agenda for the country, inviting the United States to participate wherever it can.

In contrast to the strict structural-adjustment program AID is trying to impose on Costa Rica, the program in Guatemala is more balanced between austerity measures and programs designed to maintain a certain level of social services and public investment.[5] In fact, AID has encouraged the government to increase public-sector investment in rural areas, especially in the conflictive highlands. AID, for example, is supporting a massive rural-roads programs. The primary reason for this support for public-sector infrastructure and social-services programs is a common recognition on the part of both Washington and the Guatemalan government and army that political control can be increased through such programs, most of which are closely coordinated with the army's pacification campaign. As former AID director Peter McPherson noted, AID's agenda in the highlands "is directed at the rural poor, especially the Indians" and "addresses the underlying social/economic conditions which fan insurgency."[6]

For related reasons, privatization of the public sector — a worldwide focus of AID — does not receive the same emphasis it does in other countries, such as Honduras and Costa Rica. For one thing, privatization is a sensitive issue in a country where it is the army itself that is in control of many public-sector corporations. There is also a recognition on the part of AID that the public sector has played a crucial role in moving the economy along at a time when private investment is sparse.

For the most part, U.S. foreign-policy statements parrot the distorted version of reality offered by the Guatemalan government and army. In an obvious evasion of the truth, the U.S. embassy blames leftist guerrillas, rather than the military, for the economic and social devastation of the highlands. In its 1986/87 Action Plan, the AID Mission in Guatemala made no mention of such continuing obstacles to rural development as obligatory civil patrols and military control over most aspects of rural life. AID claims that "the vitality of the cooperative movement, particularly in the Highlands, was seriously sapped during the insurgency of the early 1980s." In fact, as many army officials even admit, the cooperatives, many of which AID had helped establish, were victims of military terror. As if wearing blinders, AID asserts that the nation's economy is "ravaged by guerrilla warfare" while making no mention of the degree to which the Guatemalan economy is sapped by the military budget.

Some differences remained regarding U.S. regional policy in Central America. Guatemala, concerned more with its own internal stability and with its international standing, declined to provide the kind of support Washington wanted for its destabilization war against Nicaragua. But on the whole, there exists a strong coincidence of political and economic policies, both on the domestic and regional level.

Prospects for the 1990s

During the 1980s U.S. foreign policy backed the transition from direct military to civilian rule while at the same time increasing its support of the armed forces. Like the Guatemalan army itself, Washington recognized that the best guarantee for political and economic stability was a civilian-military alliance in which civilian political parties administered the government while the army dedicated itself to internal security. By the end of the decade, however, the limits of this policy were becoming more evident.

The "democratization" process had lost much of its earlier domestic and international credibility due to the corrupt and unprincipled behavior of the Christian Democratic government and its failure to assert civilian authority over the armed forces. The disintegration of the army's National Security and Development Plan, with its timetable for crushing the guerrilla forces and pacifying the rural population, caused cracks in the military's internal cohesiveness, resulting in several attempted coups by dissident elements. As the military's plan for national stability crumbled, human rights abuses became more widespread not only among the popular movement but also among reformist political and business leaders.

The projected decrease in the U.S. aid package in the early 1990s will further test the weak foundation of the country's economic and political stability. Budget cutbacks, competing requests for U.S. aid, and fading foreign-policy concern with Central America may mean that Guatemala will be unable to count on substantial U.S. support in coming years. This, combined with likely reductions in Western European and multilateral assistance, will aggravate political, economic, and military tensions within the country.

Although Guatemala will not be able to count on large annual commitments of U.S. aid, the stability of Guatemala will continue to concern Washington. But with less funding available and its political and economic stabilization already having proved deficient, the U.S. government may have a more difficult time influencing the country's future. In the early part of the decade, U.S.-Guatemala relations will also be tested by the often contradictory aspects of U.S. policies, including the following:

* New drug-enforcement measures—while an important source of support for the military and police—will increase tensions as the involvement of the security forces in drug operations comes to light.

* Friction experienced in the late 1970s when the Carter administration attempted to rebuke the Guatemalan military for human rights abuses may increase again as Washington begins to express concern about the deteriorating human rights climate. At the same time that Washington warns the country to reduce human rights violations it is supporting a counterinsurgency war notorious for its barbarity.

* U.S. support for economic stabilization, conservative free-market economics, and structural adjustment aggravates social tensions resulting from deteriorating socioeconomic conditions.

U.S. Trade and Investment

No other Central American country, with the exception of Panama, has attracted so much U.S. trade and investment. The United States is Guatemala's leading trading partner, purchasing 41 percent of its exports and providing 39 percent of its imports. According to the U.S. Department of Commerce, trade and investment guarantees provided by the

U.S. Eximbank and OPIC, was well as the incentives offered by the Caribbean Basin Initiative (CBI), have accelerated U.S. trade with Guatemala in the late 1980s. Most new investment has been in export-oriented manufacturing operations, mostly clothing assembly plants, and in nontraditional agricultural operations.

Except for a few years in the early 1950s when an agrarian-reform program affected the uncultivated lands of United Fruit, U.S. investors have always enjoyed a highly favorable business climate in Guatemala. Some 400 U.S. firms have investments in the country, ranging from small tourist businesses to large transnational corporations like United Brands and RJ Reynolds. Ninety of these companies are among the top 500 corporations in the United States. According to the Commerce Department, the top U.S. investors in Guatemala are Castle & Cooke, Goodyear, and Texaco.[7]

Investors in the agricultural sector are mostly small U.S. agribusiness companies involved in the production and processing of nontraditional agroexports. Many of these have received loans from an AID-financed corporation called the Latin American Agribusiness Development Corporation (LAAD). Among the better-known U.S. agribusinesses operating in Guatemala is RJ Reynolds, which owns the Del Monte banana plantations near Puerto Barrios on the Atlantic coast. Goodyear cultivates rubber plantations, and Ralston Purina runs a variety of agro-industries including a feed mill. Other food-processing giants in the country include Warner Lambert (gum manufacturing), Beatrice (snack foods), Coca-Cola (instant coffee), and Philip Morris (cigarettes).

Seventeen of the top 20 U.S. pharmaceutical firms are active in the country, as are the top ten U.S. chemical firms, which manufacture pesticides. Three hotel chains—Sheraton, Ramada Inns, and Westin Hotels—help tourists feel at home in Guatemala. All top five petroleum corporations have distribution outlets in the country. The State Department once called Guatemala "the plum of Central America" because of its potential oil reserves but the slow rate of extraction has dampened investor enthusiasm.[8]

U.S. Economic Aid

Although U.S. military aid was halted in 1977, modest levels of U.S. economic aid continued to flow to Guatemala during the Lucas García and Ríos Montt regimes. In the early 1980s, this aid—averaging about $15 million a year—was an important, and in some cases the only source of support for military-sponsored development programs in the northwestern highlands.[9] As Guatemala moved toward civilian rule in the mid-1980s, the Reagan administration successfully pressured Congress for substantially increased economic aid to Guatemala. By 1989 Guatemala had become the seventh-largest recipient of U.S. economic aid in the world.

During the 1980s Guatemala received almost $800 million in AID funding. About 50 percent of this aid came in the form of balance-of-payments support either through Economic Support Funds (ESF) or the Title I food-aid program. This downpour of U.S. dollars provided crucial foreign financial support for the institutional reordering and stabilization plan initiated by the military high command in 1984. The ESF and Title I programs were used by AID to back an economic-stabilization program for the Cerezo government and to push through such conservative structural-adjustment measures as currency devaluation and price liberalization. Besides ESF and food aid, Washington has funded Development Assistance projects and determined how the Guatemalan government expends the local currency generated by U.S. balance-of-payments support.

Aid for Counterinsurgency

AID program summaries, strategy statements, and congressional budget presentations make little or no mention of the counterinsurgency war. There are no references to the fact that the army's multifaceted counterinsurgency campaign focuses on the very same parts of the country where AID's own rural development programs are concentrated. There is no discussion of the degree to which the military determines the development priorities for the highlands and other conflictive areas. Nor is there any mention of the control that the military exercises through inter-institutional councils over the financial resources of other government agencies.[10]

Initially, AID contributed directly to the model village and development pole programs of the military regimes of Ríos Montt and Mejía Víctores. A congressional resolution in 1984 further prohibited such direct aid, but indirect funding from AID continues to contribute to the military's "development" plans for the conflictive areas. Apparently, AID has made no attempt to restrict the Guatemalan government agencies it funds from using these funds to advance military-directed development projects. Examples of this indirect flow of funds for counterinsurgency objectives include a variety of AID activities:

  * AID since 1981 has been the main supplier of food and money for World Food Program (WFP) projects in Guatemala, which provided the underpinnings for the infamous "Beans and Guns"

pacification project and for food-for-work programs that built model villages and army barracks in the highlands.

* AID is the main source of funds for rural-roads projects at a time when the army considers the construction and maintenance of penetration roads to be critical to its counterinsurgency efforts.

* Direct AID funds as well as local currency funds generated by Title I and ESF programs have flowed into the military-controlled relief organizations of the National Reconstruction Committee and the National Emergency Committee (CNE).

* Many of the government agencies funded by AID — including INAFOR, Ministry of Education, National Cooperative Institute, Ministry of Health, Rural Roads, INDECA, National Agrarian Transformation Institute (INTA), Agricultural Development Bank (BANDESA), National Housing Institute (BANVI), and the National Electricity Institute (INDE) — have been requested by the military to provide priority attention to the development poles and model villages. In this way, AID-financed community development promoters, agricultural credit, technical assistance, housing, and cooperative formation have served the army's National Security and Development Plan.[11]

Although AID is prohibited from using economic aid to support military programs, the supply of AID-donated food and housing supplies for model villages in the early 1980s violated this regulation. Also in violation is a more recent AID accord, through its Office of Disaster Assistance, to supply and train the army's National Emergency Committee community promoters in disaster response and prevention.

Nontraditional Exports, But Little to Eat

One of the most serious problems facing Guatemala, according to AID's 1986 *Country Development Strategy Statement*, is the "gradual decline in the rate of food production." For the late 1970s, the annual rate of food production was 1.6 percent below the rate of population growth. In the 1980s the state of food production and the availability of affordable basic grains have deteriorated even further.[12]

Nonetheless, AID has chosen to promote nontraditional agroexports and discourage local grain production, with the conviction that increased exports will not only ease the country's balance-of-payments situation but also create employment opportunities for the rural poor. To fill the gap created by declining per capita food production, AID has dramatically increased the levels of food aid and encouraged the country to import basic grains produced in the United States. In Guatemala, AID sponsors numerous agricultural development projects—all of which aim to promote agroexport production. These projects—including Highlands Agricultural Development, Small Farmer Diversification Systems, and Agribusiness Development—have been at least partially responsible for Guatemala's increase in nontraditional agroexports.

Private-Sector Support

In its support for the private sector, AID is caught in a contradiction. On the one hand, it acknowledges that the conservative elite has successfully blocked fiscal and agrarian reforms necessary to the country's economic and political stability. On the other hand, AID has rewarded this reactionary sector with the lion's share of its economic assistance programs. Since 1983 AID has tried to prop up and stimulate the private sector with an dizzying array of development programs, including Agribusiness Development, Private Sector Development Coordination, Private Enterprise Development, Private Sector Education Initiatives, Micro-Enterprise Development, Micro-Enterprise Promotion, and Entrepreneurial Development.

In addition, private-sector business organizations, especially those promoting export production, have been favored recipients of AID dollars. Numerous business organizations have even been created with AID funds. The private sector also stands first in line to receive local currency funds generated by AID's Title I and ESF programs.

AID's Private Enterprise Development project illustrates AID's elite approach to international development. It is a $10 million project that channels funds to the AID-created Chamber of Entrepreneurs and several other business organizations. According to AID, this is the flagship project of its "Strengthening the Private Sector" Action Plan. Part of this project is paradoxically titled "Private Sector Initiatives," though the impetus for the project comes largely from AID.

Democracy Strengthening

Soon after the Guatemalan army announced, in 1983, that it would be returning the country to civilian and constitutional rule, AID began providing essential support for this process. Most of the dollars for what AID terms "Democracy Strengthening" come not from money allocated to the AID Mission but from regional funding programs. For AID, democracy strengthening includes financing the electoral process itself, supporting public forums to discuss national issues, promoting U.S.

scholarships and civic-education programs, upgrading and financing the country's judicial system, and training police.

As with other AID projects, Democracy Strengthening, at least on paper, addresses many areas of real need. Yet, as with so many other AID projects, the money spent often ends up being counterproductive because of AID's failure to consider structural obstacles to change and development. Also undermining even the best of projects are the underlying political goals of the U.S. economic program. This has been especially true with its Democracy Strengthening programs, which, rather than promoting democracy, have furthered a political agenda by the army, which, at its heart, is antidemocratic.

In 1954 Washington directed a coup that overthrew a democratic government and installed a rightwing, military-controlled one. It followed the coup with extensive economic aid programs, intending to remake Guatemala into "a showplace of democracy." Thirty years later Washington was disbursing economic aid to support a military strategy to modernize the country's political system, the legitimacy of which was seriously questioned both domestically and internationally. This time it served Washington's interests to democratize the country's political institutions rather than militarize them. Two years after the military regime of Mejía Víctores began the democratization process, the Reagan administration called Guatemala "the most recent democratic success story in Central America."

Indeed, the democratization of Guatemala has been a success, but mostly in terms of its showcase features. The electoral process, which AID financed through the Inter-American Center for Electoral Assistance and Promotion (CAPEL), went smoothly, just as it has in El Salvador, which has served as a model for the Guatemalan democratization-counterinsurgency project. As in El Salvador, a succession of assembly, municipal, and presidential elections were held, with the promotional and logistical aspects of this process paid largely by AID and USIA.

Beyond the electoral process itself, the U.S. government has created and financed institutions designed to support this showcase of democracy. This has involved the financing of an array of study centers and forums whose objective is to popularize a language and ideology of democratization. Organizations that have received U.S. funds for democracy strengthening include the following:

The **Center for Political Studies (CEDEP)** is the most liberal of the study and propaganda centers funded by the United States. CEDEP began its existence with polling and get-out-the vote projects in 1985 and has sponsored a series of forums on such issues as the peace process and the Caribbean Basin Initiative. It has close links to the Christian Democratic party and has come under attack by the extreme right wing.

The center-right think tank **Association of Social Studies and Research (ASIES)** receives most of its funding from the Konrad Adenauer Foundation, a branch of the conservative Christian Democratic Party of West Germany. The goal of ASIES is the stabilization of democracy within the context of a joint military-government counterinsurgency project. The largest of the country's think tanks, ASIES has various functions. It sponsors forums and publishes bulletins to enhance popular education on such themes as the environment and elections. While this is the most visible part of ASIES, its main work is in behind-the-scenes formulation of policy for government and the modernizing sector of the military. It is pluralistic in the sense that it attempts to bring together a wide range of perspectives. ASIES, which includes retired military officials in its directorate, cosponsored a forum at American University in Washington in 1988 with ESTNA, the military's new political think tank.

Founded in the 1960s, the **Center for Social and Economic Studies (CEES)** is the oldest think tank in Guatemala. It is linked to the extreme political right and serves as a mouthpiece for conservative economic theories. Its Alfa and Omega Studies Collection publishes pamphlets promoting the causes of anticommunism, neoliberal economics, and the primacy of the private sector – all topics of the New Right in Guatemala. CEES is closely associated with the AID-funded Francisco Marroquín University.

In addition to supporting these three think tanks (ranging from center to extreme right), the U.S. government is also a main source of funding for study and propaganda centers serving business and conservative labor in Guatemala. The Study Center of the AIFLD-sponsored CUSG labor confederation, for example, depends entirely on USIA and AID funding. The Chamber of Free Enterprise, a branch of the economic New Right, utilizes U.S. economic aid to sponsor forums on political organizing for the business elite. Two other business organizations – Chamber of Entrepreneurs (CAEM) and Guatemalan Development Foundation (FUNDESA) – also rely on U.S. funding for publications and studies that promote the business sector's vision of democratization.

AID has also directly supported political training programs for the country's business sector and political parties. Through the National Endowment for Democracy (NED), for example, U.S. funds have been channeled to the Academy for Liberty and Justice, which is closely associated with the Solidarity Action Movement (MAS) of Jorge Serrano.[13]

The AID- and NED-funded Center for Democracy supports the U.S.-government's democratization program from its offices in Guatemala City.

AID chose the Association of the Friends of the Country (Amigos del País), a 200-year-old organization of the traditional oligarchy, to implement its popular education project for rural Guatemala. This project, called the Private Sector Education Initiative Project, publishes a newspaper called *Roots: The Friendly Voice of the Campesino* (which is produced in cooperation with the Chamber of Industry). The new AID-funded Highlands Institute, based in Quezaltenango, is one of several AID projects designed to propagate pro-U.S. and conservative political values among the most promising young Indians. The Central America Peace Scholarship program does its part by bringing young Guatemalans to the United States to acquaint them with the American Way.

U.S. Military Aid

Strong ties between the two countries' security forces were established as a result of the U.S.-sponsored coup in 1954. Support for the army's civic-action programs and its counterinsurgency campaign in the 1960s further strengthened this relationship. With the advent of the Reagan administration, Washington steadily solidified its links to the Guatemalan military. Although U.S. military aid to Guatemala still does not approach the levels received by Honduras or El Salvador, Guatemala has become a substantial recipient of a variety of U.S. military aid in recent years.

The country's police forces have also benefited from extensive U.S. aid and training. Before AID's Office of Public Safety was closed by Congress in 1974 owing to human rights violations associated with the police-training program, the U.S. government had trained over 32,000 Guatemalan police—the largest such program in Central America. The program also sponsored the establishment of a joint police-military intelligence and communications center, which has been called a "computerized death squad" by human rights monitors.

The security assistance termination provisions of the Foreign Assistance Act were never formally applied to Guatemala. The State Department did not officially identify the country as having demonstrated "a consistent pattern of gross violations of internationally recognized human rights." Nonetheless, the Guatemalan military regime in 1977 objected to considerations by the Carter administration to apply such restrictions, and declined to sign further military-aid agreements with the United States. It was the position of the Guatemalan military that drastic counterinsurgency measures were needed and it could not afford to be restricted by international human rights monitoring.

Instead, it began to seek aid and training from other sources, including Israel, Argentina, and Taiwan. It was not until 1982, the year that Ríos Montt seized power, that official relations with the United States once again began warming up. The Reagan administration sought congressional approval for renewed military aid in 1983, but it was not until fiscal year 1986 that aid officially began flowing to Guatemala. Although U.S. military assistance was discontinued between fiscal 1978 and 1985, Guatemala continued to buy arms and other military supplies from the United States during this period. During the aid hiatus, Commerce Department licenses were issued for over $100 million in military or dual-use supplies, including such items as aircraft, pistols, shotguns, and military vehicles.

After 1986 direct U.S. military aid and training (through the MAP, FMS, and IMET programs) has steadily increased, but always with the congressional restriction that the assistance be of a nonlethal variety. Recognizing that the U.S. Congress would only support military aid if couched in the language of democracy strengthening, both the civilian government and the military high command of Guatemala have pleaded that U.S. aid is essential to preserve the country's democratic process. Cerezo, for example, told U.S. lawmakers that he needed U.S. military aid not so much to fight the counterinsurgency war but to demonstrate to the military that the civilian government is on their side. Military leaders, in turn, tell Congress that U.S. military aid strengthens the hand of those within the armed forces who support civilian rule and the United States.

Won over by these arguments, Congress approved increased levels of military aid, but has also set conditions — apparently to ease its own conscience. For 1988 and 1989, Congress approved $9 million on the condition that the army respect human rights, even though human rights violations were clearly rising at the time. The level of direct military aid and training dropped to $3.3 million in 1990, with a similar level projected for 1991.

For its part, the Pentagon claimed that its "austere" assistance program in Guatemala "will contribute to regional stability by providing limited counterinsurgency materiel and training." Although technically nonlethal, U.S. military aid, which has consisted mostly of helicopters, vehicles, and aircraft supplies and support, has been exactly the type of assistance the Guatemalan army has needed to pursue it counterinsurgency war.

At the end of the decade, the Pentagon stated that its main objectives in Guatemala were to:

* Enhance regional security and assist anti-terrorist missions by improving operational capabilities of the Guatemalan helicopter fleet.

* Increase ground mobility of troops through procurement of trucks and spare parts.

* Assist Guatemalan armed forces' civic-action programs by providing medical and engineering equipment and materials.[14]

Other Military Related Aid

Aside from direct military aid the Pentagon has found a variety of other ways to support the Guatemalan military, including increased commercial sales, road-building and other military/civic action programs, and critical air transport support. Logistical air support, supplied mainly from the Palmerola Air Base in Honduras, began in 1987 and has since been repeatedly provided to assist counterinsurgency operations and military-controlled refugee resettlement operations in the Petén and in the northern reaches of Quiché. At least one U.S. pilot has died and nine airmen have been injured in several crashes resulting from these logistical operations.[15]

The United States gradually stepped up its military/civic action programs in the 1980s. The first signs of this nonlethal but counterinsurgency-related activity were the medical programs sponsored by the Tropical Medicine Program of the Jungle Warfare School in the Panama Canal Area. In November 1988, only three months after the Aguacate massacre (in which 22 campesinos were killed by the army), uniformed and armed members of the U.S. National Guard participated in a civic-action program in Chimaltenango only a short distance from Aguacate. The program, jointly sponsored by AID and the Ministry of Health, was largely a public relations effort that involved teeth-pulling and aspirin distribution by the U.S. soldiers. With the Guatemalan military providing transportation and translation services, the operation was judged a success by the National Guard. Before heading back to Honduras in a Black Hawk helicopter, a U.S. trooper wrote, in English, "Happy Day" across the wall of a village shack.

Shortly after this civic action in Chimaltenango, 40 U.S. army engineers arrived in the increasingly conflictive Sololá area to direct a major road-building project designed to give the Guatemalan army access to the isolated, guerrilla-controlled areas around Lake Atitlán. Other civic-action programs in Guatemala have involved the 475th Mobile Army Surgical Hospital and the 973rd Dental Detachment.

It was, however, the $13.8 million sale in early 1989 of 16,000 M-16 assault rifles to the Guatemalan army by Colt Industries which sent the clearest signal that relations were warming and Guatemala had decided to increase its dependence on the United States. As part of its modernization drive, the Guatemalan army was switching from reliance on Israeli arms to U.S.-manufactured weapons. Following closely on this highly controversial M-16 deal, the State Department authorized the sale of an A-37B counterinsurgency plane for a nominal sum, which critics called a giveaway. Critics also noted that these sales violated congressional restrictions and the Pentagon's own stated commitment to provide only nonlethal training and aid to the country's armed forces.

Although on a much smaller scale than previously, the United States is again training Guatemalan police forces, who are under the direct control of the military. Police are being trained under Justice Department and Drug Enforcement Administration (DEA) programs. In the last several years, DEA has steadily increased its presence in Guatemala, and now has an annual operating budget of over $1 million for the country. Guatemala has become a major transshipment point for cocaine in recent years. Encouraged by Mexican traffickers, Guatemalan farmers have increased poppy production, and the U.S. embassy now classifies Guatemala as a major poppy exporter. Marijuana is also grown throughout the country, particularly in San Marcos, the Petén, and Northern Transverse Strip, usually with the cooperation of local security forces.

According to a *Los Angeles Times* report, the CIA has recently increased its involvement with the Guatemalan army's G-2 intelligence division. The CIA is paying retainers to relatively high-ranking G-2 officers for information on regional matters as well as for help in fighting drug trafficking. The paper quoted a local source saying of the G-2: "As long as they keep doing good work, you don't ask about involvement in the killings and disappearances so often attributed to them." According to the *Times* report, the CIA has "challenged the DEA for control of the war on drugs in Guatemala."[16]

Despite the continued implication of the police forces in serious human rights violations, U.S. aid pays for a variety of police training programs both inside Guatemala and in the United States.[17] Thus far, Congress has not extended to Guatemala the same kind of waiver given El Salvador and Honduras for more extensive U.S. police training. Other police aid comes from West Germany, Venezuela, and Spain.

The presence of General Fred Woerner, then commander of the U.S. Southern Command, as an honored guest at the Guatemalan Army Day celebrations in mid-1989 marked the degree to which Washington was interested in increasing its influence and contacts with the Guatemalan armed forces. Woerner presided over a ceremony in which 32 U.S. trucks were delivered to the country's Minister of Defense.

While continuing to push for increased military aid, the Pentagon has also sought to support the Guatemalan military through more indirect forms of support, such as rearming the country's troops with U.S. weapons provided through commercial channels. In providing this multifaceted assistance, Washington hopes to maintain the Guatemalan military as a closely allied and cohesive force capable of retaining the upper hand in the counterinsurgency war. The precarious military and political situation in El Salvador presents the United States with an additional incentive to keep the Guatemalan armed forces strong and stable.

Other Foreign Interests

The predominance of U.S. aid programs in Guatemala reflects the growing concentration of U.S. trade and investment in the country, as well as its perceived geopolitical importance to the United States. The political and economic interests of other countries are also reflected in the nature and size of their aid programs.

After the United States, the leading trading partners are West Germany, Mexico, and Japan. As Guatemala's second-largest trading partner, West Germany has a natural economic interest in the country. There is a significant German population, which despite expropriations during World War II still maintains substantial interests in the country's coffee industry. Assistance from West Germany is multifaceted, and appears to encompass nearly every aspect of economic and political life. So extensive is this aid that some within Guatemala have cautioned against becoming overly dependent on West Germany, where future political changes will likely affect the continued flow of large assistance.

Since 1986 the country has received over $175 million in bilateral assistance from the West German government, not counting several training programs. Bilateral assistance has included funding and supplies (including a fleet of 120 vehicles) for the police, support for rural development in Quiché, business promotion projects, sanitation and water projects for rural areas, and technical and professional training programs.

Another important conduit of aid flows through four West German private political foundations. With the advent of the Christian Democratic government in Guatemala, the Konrad Adenauer Foundation, linked to the ruling Christian Democratic government in West Germany, dramatically augmented its aid activities. The foundation, whose politics lean sharply to the right, has been working in Guatemala for two decades, providing a steady base of financial and technical support for the Christian Democratic Party of Guatemala. Among its current projects are support for the ASIES think tank, which also receives financial support from the U.S.-based National Endowment for Democracy (NED). Linked closely to the government, ASIES seeks to "stabilize" the democratic process.

Enough financial aid flows from the Adenauer Foundation to the CGT to fund the entire central office in Guatemala City of the union confederation, which is a close ally of the Christian Democratic Party. According to a foundation spokesperson, the other union confederations are "more socialist or communist oriented."[18] Other major financial assistance supports an association of medium-sized coffee growers called FEDECOCAGUA, the Guatemalan Institute for Radio Education (IGER) which focuses on the Indian population, and the political and economics departments of the conservative Jesuit-run Landívar University. With an annual budget of four million *quetzales*, the Konrad Adenauer Foundation has arranged visits to West Germany of Guatemalan police and government officials to seek bilateral (government) aid.

Three other West German political foundations — Friedrich Naumann, Friedrich Ebert, and Hans Seidel — also sponsor programs in Guatemala, although to a lesser degree. The Naumann Foundation, associated with the centrist Liberal Party, has, since 1978, been supporting cooperative development, having helped birth CENDEC, an association of cooperatives. It also funds the Foundation for Central American Analysis and Development (FADES), and supports the development of micro-enterprises. The Hans Seidel Foundation, associated with the Christian Social Union, sponsors several development projects in Guatemala, but has no office in the country. The Ebert Foundation, associated with the Social Democrats, leans more to the political left than the other foundations, funding the small Social Democratic Party (PSD) as well as several unions and popular organizations. In addition to the political party foundations, West German money also reaches Guatemala through various church-based international assistance organizations like Miserior and Adraniet.

The Cerezo government was successful in attracting assistance from the European Economic Community (EEC), although rising human rights violations endanger the continued flow of this and other European assistance. In 1988 the EEC granted $2.7 million to the controversial refugee resettlement project coordinated by the government and army. EEC food has also been distributed in refugee relocation programs in the highlands and Northern Transverse Strip. Despite heightened EEC interest in Guatemala, European trade has substantially declined. Between 1975 and 1985, Guatemalan imports from the EEC fell from 19 percent to 13 percent of the country's total imports. Exports meanwhile dropped from 33 percent to 13 percent, as the U.S. share of Guatemala's export trade increased.

During the 1970s and early 1980s the Guatemalan military appealed to such other pariah states as South Africa, Taiwan, and Israel for military and economic assistance. As the country began to received new aid from the United States and Europe in the mid-1980s, these other sources of support correspondingly decreased.

When Guatemalan businessmen search for models of economic development, they frequently turn to Taiwan. The example of an authoritarian state with an industrial economy based on export-processing appeals to those members of the Guatemalan private sector who would like to transform Guatemala into an export platform for labor-intensive manufacturing industries. Taiwanese interest in Guatemala, however, apparently stems from foreign-policy concerns. As Taiwan's ambassador to Guatemala emphasized: "We have a political interest [in Guatemala]; the economic side is less significant."[19] Although Guatemala's exports to Taiwan have increased dramatically since 1986, the amount still pales compared with the export trade with the United States or even West Germany. Within Guatemala, the economic visibility of Taiwanese immigrants grew rapidly in the 1980s. Chinese restaurants proliferated to the extent that there is now a Chinese strip only blocks from the National Palace. Over four-dozen Taiwanese-owned grocery stores opened up for business during the 1980s, and Guatemala hosts at least 19 Taiwanese-owned factories.[20]

The Overseas Commission for Chinese Affairs in Guatemala City actively promotes increased Guatemala-Taiwan political, economic, and cultural ties. As part of a cultural exchange program, it sends 25 Guatemalans to Taiwan each year for study programs. Another source of influence is the Fu Hsing Kang College for Political Warfare in Taiwan which regularly provides instruction in psychological operations and counterinsurgency to Guatemalan military officers.

The full extent of Taiwan's economic-aid program is unknown, although it appears to pivot around technical assistance for agriculture and mining. In keeping with the strong political nature of its foreign-aid program, Taiwan's agricultural-assistance program worked closely with the military in developing the agricultural component of its model village program. Streets in the model villages named after the Republic of China testify to the close ties between Taiwan and the Guatemalan army.

Israel

For two decades, the Guatemalan army has depended on Israel for training and supplies. In return, since its founding in 1948, Israel has been able to count on Guatemala as an ally in international forums. It was not, however, until the early 1970s that Israeli military and economic assistance began flowing to Guatemala. This aid swelled in the latter part of the decade after relations soured between the United States and Guatemala. Israeli aid and influence in Guatemala ranges from technical assistance programs in the agricultural sector to labor training projects and arms sales.

Not only has Israel been a major arms supplier to Guatemala, but it also has played a key role in formulating counterinsurgency strategy for the army. The influence of Israeli intelligence and military assistance is also felt in the private sector, where many leading businessmen employ Israeli security guards.

Israel supplies Guatemala with an entire range of weaponry, including Galil rifles and Uzi submachine guns. In addition, Israelis have assisted the Guatemalan army in the creation of its own arms industry producing Galil weapons, ammunition, and armor plates for tanks. Technical assistance from Israel has facilitated the installation of a radar system at the international airport and a computer communications and intelligence system for the military.

In the agricultural sector, a scholarship program allows Guatemala government officials to study farming cooperative schemes in Israel. In the 1978-1979 period, some one thousand Guatemalans received training through this program.[21] Another aspect of its agricultural-assistance program has been implemented by an Israeli parastatal corporation called the International Agricultural Development Company (AGRIDEV), founded in the 1960s to administer Alliance for Progress-type programs in Africa and Latin America. In the late 1970s, AGRIDEV sponsored an integrated rural development project in Zacapa. According to a report in *Israeli Foreign Affairs*, "There have been longstanding suspicions that Israeli agricultural enterprises have often served as covers for military and intelligence operations."[22] In Guatemala, Israel's Fighting Youth Program, which trains soldiers in agricultural techniques employed in the establishment of border settlements, is known to have been the inspiration for the agrarian aspect of Ríos Montt's pacification strategy. Israeli agricultural-development programs in Guatemala are funded in part by AID through its regional office.

Other Israeli programs have included technical assistance for the creation of the Workers Bank, a youth-leadership program, training for cooperatives, and an extensive cultural-exchange program through the Guatemalan-Israeli Cultural Institute. One indication that Israeli-Guatemalan relations may be warming to pre-1980 levels again was the May 1990 visit by Guatemala's Foreign Minister to Israel. After signing new trade and cultural accords, Foreign Minister Moshe Arens of Israel was awarded Guatemala's Order of the Quetzal. It has been almost ten years since an Israeli official has been honored with this decoration. An *Israeli Foreign Affairs* report noted that as the prospects for increasing U.S. military aid diminish Guatemala may once again be interested in resuming Israeli military aid.[23]

Reference Notes

Introduction

1. H. Jeffrey Leonard, *Natural Resources and Economic Development in Central America* (New Brunswick, NJ: Transaction Books, 1987).
2. Jim Handy, *Gift of the Devil* (Boston: South End Press, 1984). Handy's book provides an excellent history of Guatemala.
3. Stephen Schlesinger and Stephen Kinzer, *Bitter Fruit: The Untold Story of the American Coup in Guatemala* (Garden City, NY: Doubleday, 1982); Susanne Jonas and David Tobis, *Guatemala* (New York: North American Congress on Latin America, 1974); Blanche Cook, *The Declassified Eisenhower: A Divided Legacy of Peace and Political Warfare* (Garden City, NY: Doubleday, 1981); Jonathan Fried, Marvin E. Gettleman, Deborah T. Levenson and Nancy Peckenham, eds., *Guatemala in Rebellion: Unfinished History* (New York: Grove Press, 1983).
4. Mary Jo McConahay, "Political Murder Revisits Guatemala," Pacific News Service, September 22, 1989.
5. *Regionews*, August 1, 1989.
6. U.S. Embassy, *Foreign Labor Trends: Guatemala* (Washington: U.S. Department of Labor, 1989).
7. Figures for Ministry of Health reported by Teleprensa, Guatemala City, June 16, 1988.

Chapter One

1. *Guatemala: Elections 1985* (Guatemala City: Inforpress Centroamericana, October 1985); *Democracy or Deception? The Guatemalan Elections 1985* (Washington: Network in Solidarity with the People of Guatemala, 1985).
2. For a more complete description of the PNSD, see: *La Política de Desarrollo del Estado Guatemalteco 1986-1987* (Guatemala City: AVANSCO, 1988), pp.4-5. Also see: George Black, "Under the Gun," *NACLA Report on the Americas*, November 1985.
3. This concept of "national-security civilian governments" was articulated by Franz Hinkelammert, director of the Department of Ecumenical Investigations (DEI) in Costa Rica. Cited in Guatemalan Church in Exile, *Guatemala: Security, Development, and Democracy* (Managua, 1989), p.16.
4. Guatemalan Church in Exile, *Guatemala*, ibid. This is a valuable analysis of the military's national-stability project.
5. Until 1986 the governors were usually military officers but are now all civilians.
6. Towns with populations below 20,000 elect mayors and town councils every two and a half years while those with populations between 20,000 and 50,000 hold elections every five years. The local elections in department capitals and those cities with more than 50,000 residents coincide with the presidential election.

7. "National Reorganization Presidential Address to the Guatemalan Nation," March 19, 1987. Cited in Guatemalan Church in Exile, *Guatemala*, op.cit., p.23.

8. *Guatemala 1986: The Year of Promises* (Guatemala City: Inforpress Centroamericana, 1987).

9. "La Perestroika Llega a los Marxistas Guatemaltecos," *Crónica*, February 23, 1989.

10. Interview with Mario Solórzano, May 8, 1987; Partido Socialista Democrático, *Construcción del Partido Socialista Democrático y Desarrollo del Proceso de Democratización*, n.d.

11. "Las Dos Alas del PSD Luchan por Llevarse la Rosa," *Crónica*, May 12, 1988.

12. For an excellent and more thorough description of the origins of the Christian Democratic Party, see: James Painter, *Guatemala: False Hope, False Freedom* (London: Catholic Institute for International Relations/Latin American Bureau, 1989), pp.58-78. Much of this section on the DCG is based on information and analysis in the Painter book.

13. Vinicio Cerezo, *The Army: An Alternative*, as cited in Painter, *Guatemala*, op.cit., p.72. Cerezo's essay was not the first time this road to political power was outlined by the DCG. In 1974, party leader Danilo Barillas published a small book entitled *Christian Democracy and its Position on the Army: A Call for an Historic Compromise*.

14. A commentary of the now-defunct *Siete Días* television news program, cited in *Report on Guatemala* (Guatemala News and Information Bureau), November 1988.

15. Marcie Mersky, "Empresarios y Transición en Guatemala," unpublished report for CSUCA, November 1988.

16. Raul Marin, "Guatemala: Sin Lugar Para La Paz," *Pensamiento Propio*, April 1990.

17. This analysis of Guatemalan foreign policy is largely based on an excellent study by AVANSCO: *Política Exterior y Estabilidad Estatal*, AVANSCO Cuadernos de Investigación, No. 5, January 1989. Also see: Robert Trudeau and Lars Schoultz, "Guatemala," in *Confronting Revolution: Security Through Diplomacy in Central America* (New York: Pantheon, 1986).

18. *New York Times*, May 17, 1989.

19. "U.S. Noose Around His Neck," *CERI-GUA Monthly Glance*, October-November 1989.

20. *La Prensa Libre*, November 16, 1989.

21. *El Gráfico*, November 14, 1989, cited in *CERI-GUA Monthly Glance*, October-November 1989.

22. Americas Watch, *Closing the Space: Human Rights in Guatemala* (New York, November 1988), p.104.

23. For a critique of the national dialogue see: "National Dialogue: Reconciling the Poor to their Poverty," *Entre Nos*, April 1989; *Information Bulletin* (Guatemala Human Rights Commission, USA), September 1989.

24. Americas Watch, *Closing the Space*, op.cit., p.1.

25. *Insight*, March 13, 1989.

26. U.S. Department of State, *Country Reports on Human Rights for 1988* (Washington, February 1989).

27. *Mesoamérica*, April 1989.

28. Americas Watch, *Persecuting Human Rights Monitors: The CERJ in Guatemala* (New York, May 1989), p.43.

29. Americas Watch, *Closing the Space*, op.cit.

30. "The Rebels as the Focus of Political Debate," *CERI-GUA Monthly Glance*, April 1990.

Chapter Two

1. The IPM has a cement company in the department of Progreso which is not currently operative.
2. Painter, *Guatemala*, op.cit., p.50.
3. Colonel Enríquez, in Guatemalan Church in Exile, *Guatemala*, op.cit., p.6.
4. National Forum speech, August 12, 1987.
5. For a discussion about splits within the army see: Allan Nairn, "Guatemala During the Cerezo Years," *Report on Guatemala*, September 1989.
6. "Above the Law? Civil Patrols in Guatemala," *Central America Report*, May 18, 1990.
7. Ibid.
8. Americas Watch, *Closing the Space*, op.cit., p.19.
9. *Guatemala: Elections 1985* op.cit.; Gabriel Aguilera Peralta and Jorge Romero Imery, *Dialéctica del Terror en Guatemala* (San José: Editorial Universitaria EDUCA, 1981).
10. By 1990 the URNG had a presence in the departments of Petén, Alta Verapaz, Quiché, Huehuetenango, San Marcos, Quezaltenango, Totonicapán, Sacatepéquez, Sololá, Suchitepéquez, Escuintla, Chimaltenango, and in Guatemala City.
11. International Institute of Strategic Studies, *The Military Balance 1988-1989* (London, 1988).
12. *Central America Report*, January 13, 1989.

Chapter Three

1. Traditional exports are considered cotton, sugar, bananas, coffee, beef, and petroleum. All other exports are called nontraditionals.
2. Hector Gross Spiell, "Report on Guatemala" (New York: United Nations Commission on Human Rights, January 1990).
3. Cited in "Empresarios y Transición en Guatemala," a report by Marcie Mersky for CSUCA, November 1988.
4. Thomas Melville, "Land Tenure in Guatemala," *Report on Guatemala*, November-December 1986; "Girón Lights the Fuse: Land Problem in Guatemala," *Central America Report*, July 11, 1986.
5. U.S. Agency for International Development, *Land and Labor in Guatemala: An Assessment* (Washington: Development Associates/U.S. Agency for International Development, 1982).
6. Painter, *Guatemala*, op.cit., p.36.
7. "Una República Bananera que Ha Dejado de Serlo," *Crónica*, April 7, 1988.
8. Julio Figueroa, *El Cultivo Capitalista del Algodón* (Guatemala City: San Carlos University, September 1980).
9. Robert Williams, *Export Agriculture and the Crisis in Central America* (Chapel Hill: University of North Carolina Press, 1986), pp.77-94; Tom Barry, *Roots of Rebellion* (Boston: South End Press, 1987), pp.35-39.
10. "El Oro Verde," *Crónica*, December 17, 1987.
11. U.S. Department of Agriculture, "Guatemala: Agricultural Situation" (Washington, March 1, 1989).
12. Ibid.
13. Ibid.
14. Mary Jo McConahay, "U.S. Garment Jobs Fleeing to Guatemala," Pacific News Service, May 25, 1990.

Chapter Four

1. Miguel Angel Reyes and Mike Gatehouse, *Soft Drink, Hard Labor: Guatemalan Workers Take on Coca-Cola* (London: Latin America Bureau, 1987).

2. James A. Goldston, *Shattered Hope: Guatemalan Workers and the Promise of Democracy* (Boulder, CO: Westview Press, 1989).

3. U.S. Embassy, *Foreign Labor Trends*, op.cit.

4. Gerald Michael Greenfield and Sheldon Maram, eds., *Latin American Labor Organizations* (Greenwood Press, 1987).

5. "Movimiento Sindical y Popular," *CERI-GUA Monthly Glance*, September 1988.

6. Using AID funds, AIFLD covers CUSG's $267,000 annual budget while USIA monies, channeled through AIFLD and the Free Trade Union Institute (FTUI) support CUSG's Study Center which was established in 1985 to support the democratization process. The AID Mission in Guatemala supports AIFLD through its Agriculture Production and Marketing Service Project which aims "to strengthen the capacity of farm unions to furnish needed service to their members."

7. Tom Barry and Debra Preusch, *AIFLD in Central America: Agents as Organizers* (Albuquerque: The Resource Center, 1990).

8. *Central America Report*, June 22, 1990.

9. Interview with Ismael Barrios, February 27, 1989.

10. *Central America Report*, January 12, 1990.

11. AID has financed *solidarista* training programs at the John XXIII Social School in Costa Rica and founded a regional business association, FEDEPRICAP, which promotes *solidarismo* throughout the region.

12. Gustavo Blanco, "La Paz del Silencio Obrero," *Aportes* (Costa Rica), January-April 1987; Peggy Handler, "Solidarismo: A Threat to the Labor Movement," *Report on Guatemala*, May-June 1988.

13. Interview with Joseph Recinos, May 1987; Curtin Winsor, "The Solidarista Movement: Labor Economics for Democracy," *The Washington Quarterly*, Fall 1986.

14. *Central America Report*, August 4, 1989.

15. The report, *L'Observatoire de l'Informatión et de la Liberté d' Informer dans le Monde*, was cited in *Crónica*, October 20, 1988.

16. "Guatemala: Repression and Self-Censorship, Sign of the Journalistic Profession," *CERI-GUA Monthly Glance*, 1988.

17. The main leader of SIMCOS, José León Castañeda, was one of the first reporters murdered during the Lucas García regime.

18. Interview with author, May 15, 1987.

19. The owners of *La Prensa Libre* share a common history of being reporters for the long-defunct *Nuestro Diario*, a semi-official paper in the early 1950s. In 1951, they renounced their positions when Arbenz became president and founded the current daily.

20. *Central America Report*, August 4, 1989.

21. "Réquiem por los Telenoticieros," *Crónica*, June 2, 1988.

22. U.S. Embassy, *Country Data: Guatemala* (Guatemala City, January 1, 1989.

23. UNICEF, *Dimensions of Poverty in Latin America and the Caribbean* (Washington, 1982), cited in Painter, *Guatemala*, op.cit., p.3.

24. Joseph Breault, "Health on Horseback," *Links* (NCAHRN), Fall 1988.

25. See *Links*, Summer 1986 and Summer 1987.

26. Guatemala Health Rights Support Project, *Reading the Vital Signs: Report of the 1988 Health Delegation to Guatemala* (Washington, October 1988).

27. Painter, *Guatemala*, op.cit., p.4.

28. *Crónica*, October 20, 1988.

29. Guatemala Health Rights Support Project, *Reading the Vital Signs*, op.cit.

30. Brook Larmer, "Religious Row Endangers Guatemala," *Christian Science Monitor*, March 10, 1989.

31. The following section on the Catholic church and the evangelical movement is largely extracted from the report *Directory and Analysis: Private Organizations with U.S. Connections in Guatemala* (Albuquerque: The Resource Center, 1988).

32. It is interesting to note that one priest was killed on the last day of the Laugerud government, eleven during the Lucas García regime, and one during the Mejía Víctores government. Paradoxically, there were no priests killed during the Ríos Montt regime although a few dozen evangelical pastors suspected of harboring leftist sympathies were murdered during his short tenure.

33. *The Clamor for Land: A Collegial Pastoral Letter by the Guatemalan Bishops' Conference* (Managua: Guatemalan Church in Exile, May 1988); Penny Lernoux, "Bishops Take Courageous Stand," *National Catholic Reporter*, October 7, 1988.

34. "Guatemala: Challenges to the Military Model," *Envío* (Managua), May 1990.

35. "1989: The Army Took The Civil Mask Away," *CERI-GUA Monthly Glance*, March 1990.

36. For a book-length analysis of the Catholic church, see: José Luis Chea, *Guatemala: La Cruz Fragmentada* (San José: Department of Ecumenical Investigations, 1988).

37. Roy Wingegard, "Primer Reporte General del Crecimiento y Distribución de la Iglesia Evangélica de Guatemala," January 1988.

38. Donna Eberwine, "To Ríos Montt with Love Lift," *The Nation*, February 26, 1983.

39. Larmer, "Religious Row Endangers Guatemala," op.cit.

40. *ONGs, Sociedad Civil, y Estado en Guatemala* (Guatemala City: AVANSCO/IDESAC, March 1990), p. 23.

41. *Directory and Analysis: Private Organizations with U.S. Connections in Guatemala*, op.cit.

42. *Informe Anual de Actividades: 1984* (Guatemala City: Comité de Reconstrucción Nacional, Area de Cooperación Nacional e Internacional, n.d.)

43. Interview with Heather Nesbitt, March 1987.

44. Alison Acker, "Aiding Guatemala," unpublished report, July 1987.

45. For a more complete treatment of NGOs in Guatemala see: *Análisis del Fenómeno de las ONGs* (Guatemala City: IDESAC/SERJUS/SOJUGMA, 1988); *ONGs, Sociedad Civil, y Estado en Guatemala*, op.cit., and *Directory and Analysis: Private Organizations with U.S. Connections in Guatemala*, op.cit.

46. *Informe de La Cuarta Conferencia Regional Sobre la Integración de la Mujer* (CEPAL, October 31, 1988); *Situación de la Mujer en Guatemala* (Ciencia y Tecnología para Guatemala, March 1987).

47. Luisa Frank and Philip Wheaton, *Indian Guatemala: Path to Liberation* (EPICA, 1986).

48. George Lovell, "From Conquest to Counterinsurgency," *Cultural Survival Quarterly*, Vol.9 No.2, 1985; Neil Boothby, "Uprooted Mayan Children," *Cultural Survival Quarterly*, Vol.10 No.4, 1986.

49. "Operación Ixil," *Revista Militar*, September-December 1982; Chris Krueger, "Re-education and Relocation in Guatemala," *Cultural Survival Quarterly*, Vol.10 No.4, 1986.

50. This section is based largely on the following article: Alex Michael, "Indigenous Peoples in the Guatemalan Struggle," *Report on Guatemala*, January-March 1989.

51. A statement by Jason Clay writing in *Cultural Survival Quarterly* as cited in *Report on Guatemala*, January-March 1989.

52. Interview with Carlos Guzmán Bockler, April 30, 1987.

53. *Report on Guatemala*, September-October 1986.

54. Alex Michael, "Indigenous Peoples in the Guatemalan Struggle," *Report on Guatemala*, January-March 1989.

55. U.S. Committee on Refugees, *World Refugee Survey: 1988 in Review* (New York, 1989), p.34.

56. American Friends Service Committee, *In the Shadow of Liberty: Central American Refugees in the United States* (Philadelphia, September 1988).

57. U.S. Immigration and Naturalization Service, "Enhancement Plan for Southern Border" (Washington, February 16, 1989), p.19.

58. Arthur C. Helton article in U.S. Committee on Refugees, *World Refugee Survey*, op.cit.

59. For a compilation of statements made by the CPR see: Guatemalan Church in Exile, *Offensive of the People: Campesino Against Campesino* (Managua, July 1989).

60. Communities of Population in Resistance, "Who We Are and Why We Resist," March 1989.

61. From a November 1989 speech by Archbishop Penados del Barrio, cited in *Information Bulletin*, December 1989.

62. Jim Burchfield, "Natural Resources Under Siege: The Environmental Costs of Counterinsurgency," *OSGUA Newsletter* (Chicago), Spring 1989.

63. Leonard, *Natural Resources*, op.cit., p.10.

64. Burchfield, op.cit.

65. Leonard, *Natural Resources*, op.cit., p.119.

66. Ibid., p.133.

67. Ibid., p.136.

68. Victor Perera, "A Forest Dies in Guatemala," *The Nation*, November 6, 89.

69. Leonard, *Natural Resources*, op.cit., p.94.

70. Interview with Dr. León Muniz, May 1984.

71. Bill Weinberg, *War on the Land: The Politics of Ecology and the Ecology of Politics in Central America*, unpublished manuscript.

Chapter Five

1. U.S. Agency for International Development, *Congressional Presentation Fiscal Year 1990*, Annex III (Washington, 1989), p.88.

2. For information concerning the levels of U.S. military assistance during the 1977-1986 period, see Allan Nairn, "The Guatemala Connection," *The Progressive*, May 1986.

3. For a discussion of U.S.-Guatemala relations during the Carter and Reagan administrations see: Robert Trudeau and Lars Schoultz, "Guatemala," in Morris Blachman, et.al., eds., *Confronting Revolution: Security through Diplomacy in Central America* (New York: Pantheon, 1986).

4. "A Talk by Allan Nairn: Faltan Más: During the Cerezo Years," *Report on Guatemala*, June 1989.

5. See AID's annual congressional budget presentations and U.S. Agency for International Development, *Country Development Strategy Statement FY1990-1994 for Guatemala* (Washington: December 1988).

6. Hearings before the House Subcommittee on Appropriations, April 19, 1983, p.86.

7. U.S. Embassy, *Business Fact Sheets* (Guatemala City, November 1988.

8. Tom Barry and Debra Preusch, *The Central America Fact Book* (New York: Grove Press, 1986), pp.245-248.

9. For a thorough treatment of AID support for counterinsurgency-related projects during this period, see: Tom Barry, *Guatemala: The Politics of Counterinsurgency* (Albuquerque: The Resource Center, 1986).

10. Tom Barry and Debra Preusch, *The Soft War: The Uses and Abuses of U.S. Economic Aid in Central America* (New York: Grove Press, 1988), pp.107-144.

11. Ibid.

12. Rachel Garst and Tom Barry, *Feeding the Crisis: U.S. Food Aid and Farm Policy in Central America* (Lincoln: University of Nebraska Press, 1990).

13. David Corn, "Foreign Aid for the Right," *The Nation*, December 18, 1989.

14. U.S. Department of Defense, *Congressional Presentation for Security Assistance Programs, FY1989* (Washington, 1988).

15. "U.S. Noose Around His Neck," *CERI-GUA Monthly Glance*, October-November 1989.

16. *Los Angeles Times*, May 7, 1990.

17. These included the Criminal Investigations Training Assistance Program (ICITAP), the State Department's Anti-Terrorist training program, and DEA programs.

18. Interview with Dr. Frehner, Konrad Adenauer Foundation, March 6, 1989.

19. Joel Millman, "Central America is Fertile Ground for Taiwan's Surplus," *Wall Street Journal*, July 1, 1988.

20. *La Prensa Libre*, October 10, 1988.

21. Cheryl A. Ruberberg, "Israel and Guatemala: Arms Advice, and Counterinsurgency," *Middle East Report*, May-June 1986.

22. Marshall Yurow, "Agridev: Israel's Overseas Agricultural Arm," *Israeli Foreign Affairs*, April 1988.

23. *Israeli Foreign Affairs*, June 1990.

Statistics

Population

Population:	8,857,000 (1989)[1]
Urban Population:	34.3% (1988)[2]
Population Density:	211 per sq. mi. (1989)
Annual Growth Rate:	2.8% (1988)[1]
Literacy:	50%[3]
Ethnic Composition:[3]	
Ladino:	54%
Indian:	44%
Religion:	
Catholic:	65%
Protestant:	33%[4]

Health

Life Expectancy at Birth:	62.2 years[1]
Infant Mortality per 1,000 Live Births:	79 (1988)[5]

Economy

GDP:	$9,600 million (1987)[6]
Per Capita GDP:	$1,154 (1987)[6]
Income Distribution (1980):[7]	
Poorest 20% of Population:	5.3% of income
30% Below the Mean:	14.5% of income
30% Above the Mean:	26.1% of income
Richest 20%:	54.1% of income
Rural Population in Absolute Poverty:	72% (1987)[8]

(Absolute poverty is the inability to afford food providing minimum nutritional requirements.)

Land Distribution:[9]
  2% of farms comprise 65% of farmland
  78% of farms comprise 10% of farmland

External Public Debt:	
1970:	$106 million[10]
1989:	$2,830 million[11]

Trade Balance:	-$390 million (1989)[11]
Debt Servicing as % of Exports:	24.9% (1987)[1]
External Debt as % of GNP:	34.1% (1987)[1]
Property & Income Taxes as % of Current Revenues:	13.4% (1986)[2]

Labor Force by Sector (1985):[4]

Agriculture:	58%
Manufacturing:	14%
Services:	12%
Unemployment:	13% (1988)[12]
Underemployment:	50% (1988)[13]

Top Agriculture Products as % of Total Exports (1986):[4]

Coffee	44%
Bananas	7%
Cardamom	5%
Sugar	5%

U.S. Economic Aid[14]
(millions of dollars)

	1946-1979	1980-1987	1988	1989	1990*
Development Assistance	256.0	180.2	30.0	33.3	30.1
ESF	33.7	190.7	79.8	80.5	56.5
PL480	59.2	118.3	23.4	28.3	26.5
Peace Corps	16.2	19.1	4.1	4.2	4.5
Total	365.1	508.3	137.3	146.3	117.6

U.S. Military Aid[14]
(millions of dollars)

	1946-1979	1980-1987	1988	1989	1990*
MAP	16.4	10.0	9.0	9.0	0
FMS	10.9	0	0	0	2.9
IMET	7.5	1.3	0.4	0.4	0.4
Total	34.8	11.3	9.4	9.4	3.3

* Estimated

Sources:
1) Congressional Presentation Fiscal Year 1991, Annex III, Latin America and the Caribbean, U.S. Agency for International Development; 2) Economic and Social Progress in Latin America: 1989 Report, Inter-American Development Bank; 3) World Factbook 1988, Central Intelligence Agency; 4) Europa Yearbook 1988; 5) Congressional Presentation Fiscal Year 1990, Annex III, Latin America and the Caribbean, U.S. Agency for International Development; 6) "Business Fact Sheets: Guatemala," U.S. Department of Commerce, Foreign Economic Trends, November 1988; 7) CEPAL Review, April 1984; 8) Rodolfo Maldonado, Guatemalan Minister of Labor; 9) Land and Labor in Guatemala: An Assessment, Agency for International Development, 1982; 10) World Development Report 1988, World Bank; 11) Notas Sobre la Economía y el Desarrollo, CEPAL, Decem-

ber 1989; 12) Foreign Economic Trends: Guatemala, U.S. Department of Labor, October 1988; 13) Business Latin America, January 16, 1989; 14) U.S. Overseas Loans and Grants: Obligations and Loan Authorizations July 1, 1945-September 30, 1983, U.S. Agency for International Development, Office of Planning and Budgeting; U.S. Overseas Loans and Grants: Obligations and Loan Authorizations July 1, 1945-September 30, 1987, U.S. Agency for International Development, Office of Planning and Budgeting; Fiscal Year 1991 Summary Tables, U.S. Agency for International Development.

Chronology

1676	Foundation of the University of San Carlos (USAC) in Guatemala City, the first university in Central America.
1795	Formation of Amigos del País (Association of the Friends of the Country).
1821	Central American region declares its independence from Spain.
1822	Annexation to Mexico.
1823	Independence from Mexico as United Provinces of Central America.
	U.S. pronouncement of Monroe Doctrine.
1826	Outbreak of civil war.
1830	Morazán takes Guatemala City, becomes president of United Provinces of Central America.
1839	Central American federation disintegrates.
	Guatemala claims to have inherited sovereign rights over Belize from Spain.
1850	U.S.-British treaty; Britain agrees to refrain from occupying, fortifying, or colonizing any part of Central America. Britain claims that this treaty exempts Belize as a prior settlement. Guatemala claims that it signed this treaty because the parties agreed to build a road to the Caribbean coast for Guatemala's use.
1859	Guatemala signs treaty, recognizes British sovereignty of Belize.
1871	Liberal Barrios takes power from conservatives; Catholic church suffers loss of power and prestige.
1882	U.S. missionary founds the first Protestant church which now stands in the shadow of the National Palace.
1884	Guatemala threatens to repudiate treaty of 1859.
1885	Barrios assassinated.
1894	Formation of several worker associations.
1898	Estrada Cabrera takes power.
	The first Huelga de Dolores, a demonstration by students during Holy Week which becomes an annual tradition continuing to the present, except during the Lucas García regime.
1901	The first transnational corporation, United Fruit Company, arrives in Guatemala.
1918	Formation of the Worker Federation for the Legal Protection of Labor (FOG) under the influence of the America Federation of Labor.
	President Wilson determines who will develop oil resources in Guatemala.
1920	Estrada Cabrera overthrown; United States intervenes militarily.
	Central America Unionist Party elected.
	Formation of the Guatemalan Association of University Students (AEU).

1921   With U.S. encouragement, coup installs military government.

1922   The Workers Regional Federation of Guatemala (FROG) begins organizing at United Fruit.

1929   International Railways of Central America (a United Fruit affiliate), connects its railways between El Salvador and Guatemala.

1931   Ubico elected; purge of leftists and repression of unions for the next 13 years.

1936   Britain offers £50,000 to help build the road to the coast without admitting liability, Guatemala demands £400,000.

1944   Ubico overthrown in military coup; "October Revolution" breaks out and victorious forces sponsor new elections.

1945   Reformist candidate Juan José Arévalo is elected president.

       New democratic constitution promulgated; women granted suffrage; "Belice" defined as the 23rd department.

1946   Formation of the National Committee of Trade Union Unity (CNUS).

1947   New labor code establishes the right to organize and strike.

1948   Union rights extended to agricultural workers.

1949   Francisco Javier Arana, chief of the armed forces, is assassinated soon after announcing his candidacy for president.

       Unsuccessful military coup attempt.

1950   Jacobo Arbenz Guzmán elected president.

1951   General Confederation of Workers of Guatemala (CGTG) unites all labor organizations with 100,000 total membership.

1952   Agrarian reform expropriates uncultivated estates and redistributes them to landless peasants.

       Communist Party legalized.

1953   United Fruit Company plantations and the International Railways are nationalized; 400,000 uncultivated acres are redistributed to landless peasants.

1954   CIA's "Operation Success" topples Arbenz government; Carlos Castillo Armas of the National Liberation Movement (MLN) takes power.

       Expropriated lands returned to former owners; all unions disbanded; thousands of people are killed.

       Formation of the clandestine Guatemalan Workers Party (PGT).

1955   Castillo Armas confirmed as president.

       Formation of the Guatemalan Christian Democratic Party (DCG).

1956   New constitution promulgated.

       Unions associated with ORIT are allowed to organize.

       Formation of Coordinating Committee of Agricultural, Commercial, Industrial, and Financial Associations (CACIF).

1957   Castillo Armas assassinated; Vice President Luis Arturo González named provisional president.

       Presidential elections turn into riots, military takes control of government and names Guillermo Flores Avendano as head of state.

       Formation of the Revolutionary Party (PR).

1958   New elections won by conservative Michael Ydigoras Fuentes.

1960   Failed U.S. invasion of Cuba is launched from Guatemalan and Nicaraguan soil.

1961   Belize turns down an offer to become an "associate state" of Guatemala.

       Foundation of Rafael Landívar University.

Formation of the Conference of Religious Orders of Guatemala (CONFREGUA).

1962 Formation of the M-13 and Rebel Armed Forces (FAR) guerrilla groups after a failed coup attempt by a group of reformist officers.

1963 Army removes Ydigoras and names Defense Minister Alfredo Enrique Peralta president.

Constitution replaced by a Fundamental Charter of Government.

Diplomatic relations with the United Kingdom suspended due to dispute over Belize; Guatemala threatens war.

1964 Formation of the Democratic Institutional Party (PID).

1965 New constitution promulgated.

A U.S. lawyer appointed by President Johnson mediates dispute with Belize. The proposal he presents favors Guatemala and is rejected by all parties in Belize.

1966 PR candidate Julio César Méndez Montenegro is elected president.

U.S. Special Forces participate in "Operation Guatemala," a counterinsurgency campaign led by Arana Osorio which kills more than 8,000 people.

Appearance of the White Hand and other rightwing death squads, which are believed to be responsible for more than 30,000 deaths over the next seven years.

1968 U.S. ambassador John Mein is assassinated.

Formation of the National Confederation of Workers (CNT), affiliated with the Christian-Democratic CLAT, as an alternative to ORIT-backed organizations.

1969 Formation of the Bank and Insurance Workers Federation (FESEBS).

1970 MLN candidate Carlos Arana Osorio elected president.

West German Ambassador Karl von Spreti assassinated.

1971 Formation of the Organization of People in Arms (ORPA).

Foundation of the Francisco Marroquín University.

1972 Negotiations with Britain break off; Guatemala threatens war by mobilizing troops at the Belize border. Britain sends a fleet and several thousand troops to Belize.

Formation of Guatemalan Army of the Poor (EGP).

Formation of the Army Bank by the Military Social Welfare Institute (IPM).

1973 Teachers' strike involves 20,000 people and promotes other public sector strikes.

1974 Rightwing candidate Kjell Laugerud García elected president in narrow victory over Ríos Montt.

1975 Tension with Belize prompts Britain to send a squadron of Harrier jets to Belize.

Belize takes the territorial dispute to the United Nations.

1976 Earthquake leaves 22,000 dead, one million homeless, and Guatemala City partially destroyed.

Resurgence of guerrilla activity.

Formation of the National Reconstruction Committee (CRN).

Hunger protest and lockout at Coca-Cola precipitates the renewal of CNUS.

U.S. Congress holds hearings on human rights situation in Guatemala, El Salvador, and Nicaragua.

1977 Miners march in Huehuetenango.

U.S. aid rejected by Guatemala because of human rights requirements.

	Mexico and other Latin American countries begin to shift from siding with Guatemala to solidarity with Belize in the territorial dispute.
1978	National elections leave no candidate with clear majority; PR-PID-CAO candidate General Romeo Lucas García elected president by the National Congress.
	Kekchí Indians protest land-grabbing by cattle-growers; army massacres 100.
	Bus fare hikes prompt massive demonstrations.
	Government elimination of union leaders begins.
	Oliverio Casteneda de León, a student, assassinated. The Guatemalan Association of University Students (AEU) changes its designation to include his name.
	Over 1000 Guatemalans receive cooperative farming training in Israel.
	Formation of Campesino Unity Committee (CUC), which joins CNUS.
	U.S. bans arms sales to Guatemala.
1979	ORPA launches its first military operation.
	Formation of the Democratic Front Against Repression (FDCR).
1980	The Spanish embassy is occupied by 39 protesters and is burned to the ground by security forces; Spain breaks off diplomatic relations.
	Workers win a five-year struggle against Coca-Cola.
	Security forces disappear 27 CNT leaders; repression forces most unions underground.
	Amigos del País and Guatemalan Freedom Fund hire U.S. public relations firms to launch a campaign in the United States praising the Guatemalan government.
	Guerrilla organizations, including ORPA, EGP, FAR, and the leadership of the Guatemalan Workers' Party, form alliance.
	The United Nations passes a resolution demanding the secure independence of Belize before the next UN session in 1981. No country votes against the measure; Guatemala refuses to vote.
1981	Army carries out major counterinsurgency offensive in Chimaltenango; 1500 Indian campesinos are killed in a two-month period.
	CUC goes underground.
	Formation of the Chamber of Entrepreneurs (CAEM).
	IMF agreement.
Apr.	Negotiations with Guatemala provoke riots and a state of emergency in Belize.
Sep.	Belize becomes a fully independent member of the Commonwealth of Nations (Great Britain), and joins the United Nations. Guatemala refuses to recognize Belize's independence and impedes its entry into the Organization of American States and other regional organizations.
1982	USAID distributes $15.5 in economic aid.
Jan.	Foreign Ministers of Costa Rica, El Salvador, and Honduras form the Central American Democratic Community. Guatemala and Nicaragua are excluded.
Feb.	Formation of the Guatemalan National Revolutionary Unity (URNG) by the EGP, ORPA, FAR, and the PGT Nucleus.
Mar.	PID candidate General Angel Aníbal Guevara wins national elections; a junta of army officers seizes power before Aníbal is installed.
Apr.	New junta unveils its National Development and Security Plan. The Civil Affairs (S-5) division is formed.

June	The junta is disbanded and its leader, retired General Efraín Ríos Montt, takes power.
	Ríos Montt's "Beans and Guns" counterinsurgency campaign escalates in Quiché, Alta Verapaz, Chimaltenango, San Marcos, and Baja Verapaz.
	"Voluntary" Civilian Self-Defense Patrols are formed; within two years there will be over 900,000 members.
July	State of siege is declared.
Aug.	World Council of Churches reports that the government is responsible for the death of over 9,000 people in the previous five months.
Sep.	Formation of the Council of State.
1983	Ardent anticommunist Cardinal Casariego dies; new church leader Archbishop Próspero Penado del Barrio adopts a more conciliatory tone.
	Oil exports reach record high, but drop 70 percent by the end of the decade.
	Formation of the National Union Center (UCN).
	Formation of Confederation of Guatemalan Trade Union Unity (CUSG).
	Formation of the Guatemalan Solidarista Union.
Jan.	Contadora group meets for first time to develop dialogue and negotiation in Central America; parties to the peace accords include Costa Rica, El Salvador, Guatemala, Honduras, and Nicaragua.
	United States resumes supplying spare military parts.
Mar.	State of siege lifted.
Aug.	Evangelical Ríos Montt alienates business, army, as well as the Catholic church; Defense Minister General Oscar Humberto Mejía Víctores seizes power in military coup.
	Mejía Víctores initiates "model villages" program.
	Army announces it will work to effect a transition to civilian rule.
	Censorship, secret tribunals, and the Council of State are abolished.
Sep.	Suspension of IMF agreement.
Nov.	Two AID employees killed by military; U.S. economic aid suspended.
1984	Constituent assembly convenes to formulate new constitution.
	Coca-Cola declares bankruptcy; workers occupy the plant and eventually win ownership.
	Formation of the National Coordinator of Trade Union Unity (CONUS) to help unions facing repression.
	The World Council of Indigenous Peoples accuses the military of systematic extermination of the Indian population.
	Kissinger Commission recommends $8 billion developmental aid to Central America and increased military assistance to Honduras, El Salvador, and Guatemala.
1985	Resumption of official U.S. economic and military aid.
	Reestablishment of the Democratic Socialist Party (PSD).
	Formation of the National Electric Workers Union (STINDE).
	Formation of Union of Guatemalan Workers (UNSITRAGUA).
	Formation of the Mutual Support Group (GAM) which brings international attention to the plight of the disappeared; a founder is assassinated.
Mar.	Coca-Cola plant in Guatemala City reopens after year-long occupation by workers and international pressure.

Aug.   A week of massive demonstrations sparked by inflation and increased bus fares.

Oct.   Christian Democrat Marco Vinicio Cerezo Arévalo wins national elections.

1986   Cerezo installed as president.

New constitution promulgated.

Federal and municipal government employees granted the right to organize.

Notorious Department of Technical Investigations (DIT) "disbands;" many of its members join the National Police.

Padre Andrés Girón and the Pro-Land Peasant Association lead 16,000 campesinos in a march to the National Palace to demand that the government distribute land to the landless.

A visiting UNICEF director says that five children under age five die every hour from easily preventable diseases.

Creation of the Special Commission to Aid Repatriates (CEAR), later expanded to include displaced people (CEARD).

West Germany gives over $175 million in bilateral assistance over the next three years.

Apr.   Formation of General Confederation of Guatemalan Workers (CGTG).

1987   Cotton production drops to a 25-year low.

USAID distributes over $177 million in aid.

Formation of the Labor and Popular Action Unity (UASP), an alliance of popular and labor organizations.

Feb.   Representatives from El Salvador, Guatemala and Honduras meet in Esquipulas, Guatemala for peace talks.

July   SEPAL survey shows that approximately 31.6 percent of all Guatemalans are evangelical.

Aug.   Presidents of Costa Rica, El Salvador, Guatemala, Honduras, and Nicaragua sign Esquipulas II peace accord.

Sep.   Formation of the National Reconciliation Commission (CNR).

Nov.   Esquipulas Accords go into effect.

Representatives from the government and URNG representatives meet in Madrid.

Army massacres 22 peasants in Aguacate and blames it on guerrillas.

Military announces "Year's End" offensive to wipe out insurgency.

1988   Cardamom market becomes saturated, nearly half the country's producers are unable to sell their crop.

AEU reports that at least seven USAC students have been kidnapped and murdered.

Formation of the Runajel Junam Council of Ethnic Communities (CERJ).

Formation of the National Coordinator of Guatemalan Widows (CONAVIGUA); Rigoberta Menchú becomes its well-known spokesperson.

Catholic bishops release a pastoral letter entitled "The Cry for Land."

Jan.   Continued Esquipulas peace talks in San José, Costa Rica.

INS reports that asylum applications from Guatemalans have risen 900 percent over the previous year; apprehensions of Guatemalans have risen 38 percent.

Mar.   "Year's End" offensive called off after major casualties incurred and failure to stamp out guerrillas becomes obvious.

Costa Rican President Arias accuses countries of Guatemala, El Salvador, Honduras, and Nicaragua with not complying fully with the Esquipulas Accords.

Apr.   Government makes a pact with UASP to increase wages and freeze prices.

URNG delegation visits Guatemala after years in exile.

The five Central American vice-presidents meet in San José to discuss the Central American Parliament and agree to present a regional economic cooperation plan to the United Nations.

May   Abortive military coup attempt.

Government-UASP pact broken.

Offices of La Epoca firebombed.

Guatemala accuses Costa Rica of noncompliance with the Esquipulas Accords because it has failed to ratify the treaty to create the Central American Parliament.

Formation of a Permanent Joint Commission with Belize.

Aug.   Another failed coup attempt.

Regional peace talks postponed twice.

Oct.   Union organizing at the Army Bank leads to death of FESEBS leader Carlos Godoy.

Nov.   Central American presidents agree to meet in January for peace talks.

Dec.   Council on Hemispheric Affairs places Guatemala at the top of its list of worst human rights offenders in Latin America.

1989   Emergence of "Jaguar of Justice," a new death squad.

Colt Industries sells 16,000 M-16 assault rifles to the army.

URNG announces that it is inflicting seven casualties a day and hopes to raise it to 15 per day by the end of the year.

PGT formally incorporated into the guerrilla coalition URNG.

Feb.   Kentucky National Guard participates in civic-action program a short distance from the site of the Aguacate massacre.

Esquipulas peace talks held in El Salvador after four postponements; Guatemala, El Salvador, Honduras, and Nicaragua say they will go ahead with the Central American Parliament without Costa Rica, whose Congress has not yet ratified the plan.

Mar.   URNG and the National Reconciliation Commission (CNR) sign accord in Oslo to initiate a three-step (political parties, social sectors, and government/military) dialogue over next several months.

May   Failed coup attempt.

1990

June   Accord signed at El Escorial, Spain between URNG and nine political parties which commits participants to work toward political solutions to the conflict.

Nov.   First round of presidential elections scheduled, to be followed by a second round in January 1991 if needed.

1991   New president scheduled to take power.

Sources for the chronology include: Encyclopedia of the Third World (1987); Conflict in Central America (Longman Group Ltd, 1987); Crisis in Central America: Regional Dynamics and U.S. Policy in the 1980s (Westview Press, 1988); Labor Organizations in Latin America, Gerald Greenfield and Sheldon Maran, editors (Greenwood Press, 1987); and "Facts of the Matter" (Central America Education Project, Summer 1987).

Bibliography

The following periodicals are useful sources of information and analysis on Guatemala:

Enfoprensa: Information on Guatemala (Chicago), weekly, English and Spanish.

Guatemala: Central America Report, Inforpress Centroamericana (Guatemala), weekly, English and Spanish.

NACLA Report on the Americas, North American Congress on Latin America (New York), bi-monthly, English.

Pensamiento Propio, Coordinadora Regional de Investigaciones Económicas y Sociales (Managua), monthly, Spanish.

Report on Guatemala, Guatemala News and Information Bureau (Oakland), quarterly, English.

Update on Guatemala, Committee in Solidarity with the People of Guatemala (New York), bi-monthly, English.

The following books and reports contain valuable background on many issues important to understanding Guatemala:

Sheldon Annis, *Gift of the Devil: A History of Guatemala* (Boston: South End Press, 1984).

Tom Barry, *Guatemala: The Politics of Counterinsurgency* (Albuquerque: The Resource Center, 1986).

George Black, with Milton Jamail and Norma Stoltz Chinchilla, *Garrison Guatemala* (New York: Monthly Review Press, 1984).

Robert M. Carmack, ed., *Harvest of Violence: The Maya Indians and the Guatemalan Crisis* (Norman: University of Oklahoma Press, 1988).

Directory and Analysis: Private Organizations with U.S. Connections in Guatemala (Albuquerque: The Resource Center, 1988).

Jonathan Fried, Marvin E. Gettleman, Deborah T. Levenson, and Nancy Peckenham, eds., *Guatemala in Rebellion: Unfinished History* (New York: Grove Press, 1983).

James A. Goldston, *Shattered Hope: Guatemalan Workers and the Promise of Democracy* (Boulder: Westview Press, 1987).

Guatemala: Security, Development, and Democracy (Managua: Guatemalan Church in Exile, 1989).

Jim Handy, *Gift of the Devil: A History of Guatemala* (Boston: South End Press, 1984).

Susanne Jonas and David Tobis, eds., *Guatemala: And Victory is So Born, Even in the Bitterest Hours* (New York: North American Congress on Latin America, 1981).

Beatriz Manz, *Refugees of a Hidden War: The Aftermath of Counterinsurgency in Guatemala* (Albany: State University of New York Press, 1987).

Michael McClintok, *The American Connection, Volume II: State Terror and Popular Resistance in Guatemala* (London: Zed Press, 1985).

Messengers of Death: Human Rights in Guatemala, November 1989-March 1990 (New York: Americas Watch, 1990).

James Painter, *Guatemala: False Hope, False Freedom* (London: Catholic Institute for International Relations/Latin America Bureau, 1989).

La Política de Desarrollo del Estado Guatemalteca 1986-1987 (Guatemala City: AVANSCO, 1988).

Política Exterior y Estabilidad Estatal, AVANSCO Cuadernos de Investigación No. 5 (Guatemala City: AVANSCO, January 1989).

Stephen Schlesinger and Stephen Kinzer, *Bitter Fruit: The Untold Story of the American Coup in Guatemala* (Garden City, NY: Doubleday, 1982).

Jean Marie Simon, *Guatemala: Eternal Spring, Eternal Tyranny* (New York: Norton, 1987).

For More Information

Resources

Centro Exterior de Reportes Informativos sobre Guatemala (CERI-GUA)/
Weekly Briefs, Monthly Glance, Special Reports
Apartado Postal 74206 C.P. 09080
Delegación Iztapalapa
México D.F., México

Committee in Solidarity with the People of Guatermala/Update on Guatemala
225 Lafayette Street, Room 212
New York, NY 10012

Enfoprensa/Information on Guatemala
4554 N. Broadway, Suite 204
Chicago, IL 60640

Guatemala News and Information Bureau/Report on Guatemala
P.O. Box 28594
Oakland, CA 94604

Inforpress Centroamericana/Infopress, Central America Report
9a Calle "A" 3-56, Zona 1
Ciudad de Guatemala, Guatemala

Latin America Bureau
1 Amwell Street
London, England EC1R 1UL

Peace and Justice

Central America Resource Center
P.O. Box 2327
Austin, TX 78768

Comité Pro Justicia y Paz de Guatemala
Apartado Postal 57-135, C.P. 06500
México, D.F., México

Guatemalan Church in Exile
Apartado Postal 1395
Managua, Nicaragua

International Labor Rights Education and Research Fund
110 Maryland Avenue NE, Box 68
Washington, DC 20002

Network in Solidarity with the People of Guatemala (NISGUA)
1314 14th Street NW #17
Washington, DC 20005

Peace Brigades International
Calle Mariscal 10-10, Zona 10
Ciudad de Guatemala, Guatemala

Women for Guatemala
P.O. Box 53421
Washington DC 20009

Human Rights

Americas Watch
1522 K Street NW, Suite 910
Washington DC 20005

Amnesty International
322 8th Avenue
New York, NY 10001

Comisión de Derechos Humanos en Guatemala/International Bulletin
Apartado Postal 5-582 C.P. 06500
México D.F., México

Guatemala Human Rights Commission, USA
1359 Monroe Street NE
Washington, DC 20017

National Central America Health Rights Network/Links
P.O. Box 202
New York, NY 10276

Tours

Center for Global Education
Augsburg College
731 21st Avenue South
Minneapolis, MN 55454

Business/Official

Embassy of Guatemala
2220 R Street NW
Washington DC 20008

Embassy of the United States in Guatemala
APO Miami, FL 34024

Fundación para el Desarrollo de Guatemala (FUNDESA)
Edificio Cámara de Industria, 9 Nivel
Ruta 6, 9-21, Zona 4
Ciudad de Guatemala, Guatemala

U.S. State Department
Citizen's Emergency Center/Travel Information
Main State Building
Washington DC 20520
(202) 647-5225

Country Guides

If you really want to know Central America — get the whole set!

Only $9.95 each

To Order:
Each order must include $2.00 postage and handling for the first book,
and 50¢ for each additional book up to six books.
(Please contact us for postage and handling charges for delivery outside the U.S.)

Discount:
When ordering all seven books, postage and handling is free!

Please request a free catalogue of publications

The Resource Center
Box 4506 * Albuquerque, New Mexico * 87196

More Resources

The Central America Fact Book
by Tom Barry & Debra Preusch
One of the best guides to understanding the economic and political situations in each country of the region.
Paperback, Grove Press, 1986.

Roots of Rebellion: Land and Hunger in Central America
by Tom Barry
A critical study that looks behind the news flashes of earthquakes and coups to the real crisis in Central America: land and hunger.
Paperback, South End Press, 1987.

The Soft War: The Uses and Abuses of U.S. Economic Aid in Central America
by Tom Barry & Debra Preusch
This groundbreaking work closely examines the many U.S. government agencies involved in pacification, stabilization, and low-intensity conflict programs in the region.
Hardcover, Grove Press, 1988.

Please request a free catalogue of publications

**The Resource Center
Box 4506 * Albuquerque, New Mexico * 87196**